Hair Al

An account of my youth and early manhood

By
Jago Hayden

Dedicated to those who were there for me.

Published by Black Lion Books,
Crannoge Boy, Loughros Point, Ardara, Co. Donegal, Ireland

PUBLISHED 2000

ISBN 0-9539372-0-8

Enquiries to:

Black Lion Books,

Crannoge Boy, Loughros Point, Ardara, Co. Donegal.

Telephone: 075-41215   E-mail: jagohayden@eircom.net

Printed by e print limited.
105 Lagan Road, Dublin Industrial Estate, Glasnevin, Dublin 11.
Telephone: +353-(0)1-830 4141   email: books@eprint.ie   web: www.eprint.ie

Cover Picture by Stephen Bennett, Ardara.

Portrait of author by Donnelly Studios, Donegal.

ACKNOWLEDGEMENTS

There are too many people who have helped me in the preparation of this book for publication to thank them all by name. However, there are a few whose contribution deserves special mention. In particular, I would like to thank Liz Prior, Noelle Campbell and Ailis Conneely for helping with the preparation and typing of the manuscript; my brothers and sisters, Billy, John, Kathleen, Eileen and Declan for fact checks; Barney for still being there; my cousin Louie for permission to write part of her personal story; Teddy Tucker for clarifying the sudden death of his father and the tragic drowning of his cousin, both in 1939; John Connolly for confirming and refreshing my memory of his grandmother's cottage; Derek Paine, for correcting my remembered version of the name of the Money River; Breda Reynolds for her gentle concern that I get my facts correct, lest I offend anyone, may she have joy in Heaven; the Irish Christian Brothers for their extraordinary input to the community I grew up in; the archivists of the Brothers, the Holy Faith Nuns, and Wicklow County Council, for their courtesy; Tony and 'Trish' O'Callaghan for their time and patience in editing my manuscript.

There were others who took my phone-calls and wrote to me; my thanks to them also for their consideration. But my work is a book of memory and that's how it must stand.

Finally, my love to my wife, Ann, who put up with my writing late and early, and my humours.

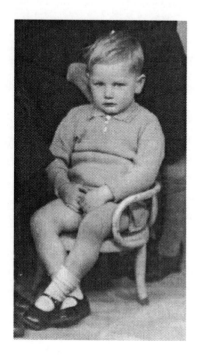

Jago Hayden, aged 2$\frac{1}{2}$,
pictured in his new button-strap
shoes for going to school.

FOREWORD

A Journey which began in County Wicklow in 1937 and has now, in the new century, reached Donegal, may not seem much of an adventure. Take the road to Sligo and you'll do it in three or four hours. But take the scenic route, via the North Sea, Norway, Russia, Tanzania, Canada, Chile and Iceland, with the odd detour to Iran and Uraguay, and it takes longer. A lifetime in fact. And it is the story of that lifetime that Jago Hayden tells in "Hair all Curling Gold".

But although, in the richness of these experiences, he is relating an adventure, the books' recurring image is of the trail that leads back from those far-off lands to the place where he was reared, a little stretch of coastline in County Wicklow, between Bray Head and Wicklow Head. He explains why this should be by a metaphor of his own, one which springs from his lifetime love of the sea and seafaring. He tells us that when your ship pulls away from the dock, eddies are drawn along with it by the friction of the hull's passage through the water, so that even at an ocean's span away, some of the harbour-water from the port of departure goes with you. And it is clear from his modest account of these adventures that whatever ocean he sailed, whether scouring the North Sea for oil, or as a Fisheries Officer in Tanzania, the waters of the Irish Sea by Greystones and Kilcoole went with him. You have the sense that, like that other tough old sailor, Ulysses, the real voyage of hope, the real adventures, were on his journey home.

I am a later arrival to that stretch of coast between Windgates and Leamore Strand. A blow-in. And the people I brought there, Miley and Biddy, Dinny and Teasy, Mary and Dick, never really existed. Even the place I brought them to, Glenroe, never existed. I had to borrow Kilcoole. People argue about how true to life they are, but there can be no quarrel about Jago Hayden's people, not just his own family, but all those who peopled his early years.

Beezie Whiston, Blacktop Kinsella – who could invent such names?

But of course, he has the advantage of me, because they really lived. And thanks to this book they will go on living.

Wesley Burrowes

PREFACE

There was a man whose house and garden backed on to the patch of common ground at the 'Rock' in the village of Kilcoole. The village is better known to this generation of Irish TV viewers as 'Glenroe' from the soap of the same name. I can't tell you the man's name, because although I'm certain I once knew it, the thing that happened is so far back that his name has faded totally from my mind. There is one word however that instantly unlocks the particular memory - pea-stakes!

Every year at springtime this man cut a bundle of stout hazels or black sallies to use as pea-stakes in his garden; or so it seemed. He didn't just push them into whatever bed he had prepared for peas that year however, but laid them carefully against his back fence, butts out, to season. When they had hardened off he erected them as a new fence along the line of the butts, gaining something over half a yard of ground in the process. So one of my pals maintained, and when we talked of him we referred to him simply as pea-stakes.

In midlife I came to live near the town of Ardara in West Donegal. I had already become, as it were, an apprentice Donegalman, having earlier moved from England to Falcarragh on the edge of Donegal's Northwest Gaeltacht - there to live, and to Gweedore for work - and had been made redundant. The bitter experience of my parents being sold out in their midlife and having to move away to England left black iron in me, and when I was made redundant in Gweedore I dug my heels in and stayed where I was. I drew the dole. I butchered pork and packed it for people with freezer cabinets. I did planning applications, drew site maps, even drew out house and chalet plans. But eventually I needed to do more and got a job in a trawl factory in Killybegs. I had to move house.

It was impossible to buy a house or a site in Killybegs. The herring fishing in the North Sea was closed. Herring prices in Ireland were astronomically high. Killybegs fishermen made a year's money in a month. Whatever property came on the market, whether house or land, was bought up by fishermen hiding money on the taxman. I found rented accommodation outside the ten-mile distant town of Ardara. A scenic place, but remote. A nearby land-holding came on the market; fourteen acres in two parcels; one of approximately four acres touching both the shore of Loughros Beg bay and the main access road, the other, ten acres of a rundale strip 'out the hill'. A too-friendly bank manager lent me the money and I bought the land. My planning application for a somewhat over ambitious two-storey house, below the road, was turned down.

I had, to my cost, ignored the prior history of confrontation between the previous owner and the planning office. Eventually, the chief planning officer of Donegal County Council came out on site to me, and agreed to consider an application for a house on a strip that had some one hundred and seventy feet of frontage, but was no more than fifty eight foot deep at any part. It had, moreover, a massive bank of rock butting in from the rear.

I built an eighty six foot house with the rock encroaching to within eighteen inches of my back door and I spent years with a lump hammer and chisels, a pick and a few wedges, quarrying away at the rock, and pulverising it then with a sledge-hammer. Meantime I set about tidying up the ditches and banks that bordered the site. It was squeezed from behind by an old roadway of considerable width that was used by neighbours tending cattle and animals on the hill, and by a couple of men that had built bungalows just to the west and to the rear. Although the road bed was wide, the carriageway lay to the near side; and because the whole sat directly on the rock which sloped slightly to the front; and because traffic created great pools that cars were steered around; I felt the original boundaries of my site had been eroded and encroached on over the years. The old ditches had further been trampled down by animals because the strip had been too long neglected. I therefore restored them, building sods on the outside, determined to gain back ground.

When my best man, a friend of many years, came with his wife to visit, I showed him what I was doing. His comment was instant. Pea-stakes!

That is how life is. We carry with us the trivia of childhood and find it resonates in some action of ours in our 'maturity'. When a ship pulls away from the dock one can see eddies being drawn along with it by the friction of the hull's passage through the water, no matter how well-faired the hull. Who is there to say when that ship reaches it's destination, even were it to be an ocean's span away, that some of that port of departure's harbour-water has not been carried across the ocean also.

Eight years before I was born a succession of easterly storms raised savage scouring seas that washed away a strong shingle beach north of Greystones Harbour, and with it a roadway and an entire row of houses that fronted the beach. The storm even breached what most people would have considered impregnable, the very harbour wall itself. When I think of the houses, and their owners and occupiers, I am minded of the poem by the blind Irish poet Raftery about a great drowning at a place called 'Anach Chuain' in County Mayo. One of his lines emphasised the scale of the tragedy by saying "nar bheag an tabhacht duinn beirt na triuir" - "---- of little importance to us two or three".

The scale of the disaster in Greystones was comparable with the tragedy of Anach Chuain but without the loss of life. But, by the time I came of an age to be aware of it, it had already been folded away into memory and I learned little of it. That was odd because the landlord of the house I was born in, a man by the name of Sam Evans, was one of those whose houses were washed away. Two brothers of his, and another near neighbour, Bert Curling, also lost their properties, and the row of adjacent bungalows in Blacklion where I was born and reared, almost a mile from the shore, were presumably built with some measure of support from their church community. They were all members of the local Church of Ireland congregation.

There were others who lost everything in the disaster also, among them my mother's Uncle Willie and his family. These were later housed in one of the older cottages in Blacklion. But however or wherever they were all housed, their loss was seemingly absorbed with a terrible fatalism. The one local tragedy that appeared to shatter that stoicism was the death of a man named Charlie Leary, the man in the well. A plumber, he was carrying out repair work to the lining of a well when a boulder got dislodged and trapped him by the leg, jamming it against a rung of a ladder. After days of attempts to dig down to him, it was decided to saw through the rung, but only Charlie Leary himself could reach it. My mother's account had it that he accidentally sawed his leg off instead. The leg was so numb he didn't feel it, and he died from loss of blood. His December death and funeral made the national papers, but we would never have known had our mother not told us.

The two Sugarloafs, with the Hill of the Downs and Coolegad Hill were the back wall of our world. Bray Head, and behind it, Killiney and Howth Head, bounded us to the north; in the distance, Wicklow Head to the south. The Irish Sea, to the east, was our morning window. Our's was a town of some fifteen hundred people. The entire area out to Newcastle and Newtownmountkennedy might have mustered five thousand. How many of these did we know? In a sense, all of them; in reality, I suppose six or seven hundred, maybe a thousand. But whether we knew them less or more was no matter, it was just important for us that they were there, and we grew in their shadow.

In the world beyond, defences more formidable than our bit of a harbour wall were readied for coming storms, and when the assaults came, succumbed just as easily. It was as if the fate of this community presaged the destiny of that wider community of nations. But as a youngster I knew nothing of this. I was born only in 1937. I was a listener though, endowed with a precocious memory, and with eyes that I was told often enough "saw far too much".

Throughout my life I have talked frequently about the things that befell me and have often been asked "when are your writing the book, Hayden?" Well, I have attempted it. If you come with me through it's pages you will meet character after character whose names you don't know and may feel therefore they don't matter. Mark them well, however. There were others like them in your lives also, and in a sense I have remembered for all of us. Mine left an eddy about my own hull that still clings a lifetime's voyage later.

Some of them were significant for reasons that I scarcely admit even to myself. Blacktop Kinsella, a Grand-Uncle whose given name was John Thomas, was a great hulk of a man, probably the biggest man, physically, in the whole area. He was the bogey man our mothers threatened us with. Those who ventured uninvited into his coalyard could expect a welt of his belt buckle - or the threat of it. But for me he is probably significant because his was the first corpse I ever saw, when he died in 1946. Not my first encounter with death. That was at the funeral of my father's cousin, Joseph Donohoe, when the crack of the rifles being fired in salute outside Kilquade church frightened the daylights out of me. By contrast, Blacktop's two sons, Jim and Jack, although both big men and physically rugged, as was their only sister Kitty, were gentle in their demeanour in a way that is not now common. It is their conversations with men that went to fish with them, that I listened to from an early age, when I accompanied my father. They, or others like them, had a great expression when they wanted to be sure you had grasped the point of whatever story they were telling: "Have you me now?"

Read on.

CONTENTS

Chapter One - I Hate Golf

Let me say it right at the start; I hate golf, utterly and totally. I hate the goddamned all-importance of it. I hate the ambience of privilege and exclusivity that goes with it. I hate the seeming need to wear shirt and jersey badges, as if those who play it can be identified only by these. I hate its cultivation of business links and its thereby intrusion into the lives of us who want nothing to do with it. I hate the inference that it is the alpha and the omega of social life. I hate its sheer seductiveness. But, most of all, I hate golf because my wife plays it.

The funny thing is, my hometown of Greystones in County Wicklow was regarded as a great place for golf, what with there being two local clubs - Greystones Golf Club itself, and a further club nearby in my father's village of Delgany - and something like half a dozen home-grown professionals. To some, Greystones was a toffee-nosed place. I'm certain the core membership of the Greystones club was drawn from those who lived on the very uppercrust Burnaby estate that abutted the town and adjoined the golf course. But there was also a solid corps of 'artisan' members who lived in strings of soldier's cottages and council houses that, broadly speaking, skirted the farther boundaries of the golf. In our time it was always called either the golf links, or simply 'the golf'. These men were readily recognisable on a Sunday morning at eight o'clock mass. They invariably stood at the back of the church and left before the 'prayers after mass'. The switching of the time of the early service, from eight o'clock to seven o'clock, every summer was probably done more to convenience them that to facilitate any visitor. But they were dedicated. I've been told the 'artisan' golfing movement started in Delgany, but if it did, it was before my time and I can't tell you about it.

We had golfing connections on both sides of our family. My Uncle Bernie's wife, May, was an aunt of Harry Bradshaw, and she herself worked in Delgany golf Club before she was married. My first cousin, Ray Hayden - his father, Mick, was an older half-brother of my father's - was the first youth in Ireland to win the 'Boy Championship' three years running. It was an achievement that has to my knowledge been matched only once since then. He became assistant professional at Woodbrook Golf Club, then later moved to the United States as a teaching professional. The family lore at the time had it that it was the famous South African golfer, Bobby Locke, who arranged this for him. Arthritis caught up with him, and the last time I met him, at his brother Ollie's funeral, he was working as a barman in New York.

On my mother's side, her uncle, Willie Kinsella, was head green-keeper at Greystones Golf Club for twenty-seven years and in my time his nephew Jack Kinsella also worked there. Yet another Kinsella, Jimmy, the Skerries professional was related as well; but Skerries was a distant place and we never met. I suppose about half our pals from school caddied at one or other of the two golf clubs as did Willie Kinsella's two sons, Michael and Billy, but nobody in our family ever did. Well, John maybe, once or twice. Our mother thought it was somehow beneath us. My only acquaintanceship with the golf links was to sleigh down the steep slope on the Crowabbey side in winters when there was snow. Golf was not a part of our lives.

My greatest friend from the time my parents were sold out by the taxman and moved to England, Jimmy Smullen, was a great all-round sportsman, having played Gaelic, Hurling and Soccer in his time. He never got into the rowing, although he had the length for it - he was something over six foot two and maybe not quite six foot four. But he became a very useful golfer, with a set of long left-handed clubs. I can remember him telling me about a charity match between Harry Bradshaw and Ray Hayden on what was their original home course, Delgany Golf Club. Ray would just step up to the ball and hit it, without appearing to study-up. More than once, he let fly with a great whoop, to the delight of the locals. I believe it was a matchplay game, but Jimmy Smullen had it tallied at 64 - a course record - for Ray, 67 for Harry. My uncle Bernie told me of another charity match involving Harry Bradshaw, this time pitted against Bobby Locke, on the long defunct Kilcroney Golf Course. The year, I think, was 1947. Bobby Locke was about to putt on the 17th. or the 18th. green - I disremember which I was told - when Bernie spotted Harry's father among the spectators on the edge of the green. Daring to do what no one involved in golf would have attempted, such was Bobby Locke's reputation, he interrupted the great South African and introduced Harry's father. At Bernie's funeral, I virtually bumped into Harry Bradshaw at the gate of the church while we were waiting for the coffin and the wreaths to be loaded into the hearse. I introduced myself and recounted Bernie's account of that particular incident. Harry immediately confirmed it, saying that Bobby Locke had never met his father before, and went on to give me the score and the result of the match.

My own liking was for Jimmy Martin, whom I met on odd occasions. From Killincarrig or the Mill Road, I'm not sure which, he was closer in age to me than the others, knew me by my family nickname of Jago, and always said hello. I chanced to meet him once when I was in the "Wicklow Arms" in my father's village of Delgany. I think I was having a drink with my Uncle Bernie, and it must have been the summer after I came back from Scotland where I had been a relief seaman on both a fisheries research vessel and a fishery cruiser. Jimmy was not long back from Scotland where he had won the Penfold tournament. It seemed to be a favourite competition of his, and he usually got into the prize money. This time, he had scooped the top prize of a thousand pounds. I told him how delighted I had been to read of it.

"Not half as delighted as I was, me oul' son, Jago", was his instant reply. One word borrowed another and we ended up talking about Scotland and what I had done up there, and about Edinburgh.

In the summer of 1960, when I first went up to Scotland, I was doing a strong line with a tall beautiful girl from Birmingham, named Claire, whom I met when she was on holiday in Greystones in 1958. That was the time I was lucky enough to get in on the first "Skipper Training Scheme". In betweentime, I had her over to Greystones, and down to Bushey, near Watford, just outside of London, where my parents were living. She was Church of England with a leaning to Methodism, and I was R.C. and in that time, this was a problem for us. When I was away on the fishery cruiser, stationed up on the Moray Firth, she met and fell for another fellow, called Mike, and thinking he couldn't be a Catholic, wrote to me and broke it off.

Jimmy Gillies, leading seaman, was the one who collected the post in the village of Cromarty that morning in the Zodiac and, at the same time, took ashore the outgoing mail. The big J.Arthur Dixon postcard addressed to her that I sent ashore with him, he might as well have thrown in the tide. When the ship docked again at Leith, our base port, I discovered a ceili out at the Embassy Ballroom at Dalkeith, and went Scottish country dancing for consolation.

The ceilis in Dalkeith were on Saturday nights and, I learned from the people I met there - all members of the Scottish Country-Dance Association, the men bedecked in full kilt regalia, and the ladies in long tartan dresses - that there was also a ceili on Tuesday nights in the Assembly Rooms at Leith. As I told Jimmy Martin about my dancing, and about my wandering down the back streets between Leith and Edinburgh, he was alarmed and asked did I not find Edinburgh a dangerous place. "What's the thing that strikes you most about Waverly Station?" he asked. "That there's always a policeman on the platform", I answered. To tell the truth, the most notable thing for me at Waverly Station was that the train had pulled

4

in to the second of the scheduled time - my first such experience - at a quarter to six in the morning, after the overnight journey from London's Kings Cross.

"Yes", said Jimmy, and went on to tell how Norman Von Nida, the Belgian golfer, was asked for the time on the platform, then had his elbows pinned from behind, his wallet lifted and he tumbled to the ground in one instant operation, after he had inadvertently flashed a wad of notes - winnings from some tournament - as he bought a farewell round of drinks in the North British Hotel just up from the station.

The last time I met Jimmy Martin was in Fitzgerald's Hotel in Bundoran. I was working at the time in G.T. Carpets in Gweedore. We had run a most successful dinner dance at Christmas in Mary Joe's "Radharc an Eargail" hotel in Derrybeg and, with the profit from the dance, had decided we should have a works outing. It was 1972 and, with the Troubles, nobody wanted to go in to the North. When I had been knocking around at the fishing, I had on two occasions got a lift with the Ritchie Fitzgerald Ceili Band and had been told that they had a small hotel/guest house in Bundoran, and if I was ever passing through, to be sure to call. I suggested Fitzgeralds and Bundoran for the outing and so it was. I'm not sure if we included the staff from Snath Comer to boost the number of girls - it's like a dream to me that we did something like that - and we arranged to run a couple of heats of the Cailin Gaelach competition during the outing. Barney Fitzgerald arranged for the band to play for us during the afternoon and suggested that, as a Pro-Am was being played at the Great Northern Hotel links that afternoon, and he knew a couple of the professionals, he could ask one of them to act as judge for us. Jimmy Martin and Jimmy Kinsella did the trick. Jimmy Kinsella was a cousin of my mother's and that was the only time I ever met him. The outing was a great success. I remember only bits of it. Ritchie Fitzgerald himself came and played for us. John Mór, stepping back out of someone's way on the little dance

5

floor, a glass of whiskey in his hand, caught that tricky place behind the knee on the edge of a table, performed a perfect backwards somersault and landed on his feet without spilling one drop of whiskey.

On the coach on the way home, a beautiful red-haired girl named Margaret Gallagher, who was sitting behind me, reached her arm around my neck and declaring: "Is gradh liom thú, Seamus Hayden", snogged me mercilessly. All the whiskey I was bought finally got the better of me and they had to stop the bus more than once on the long haul home up through Leitir-Mac-a 'Bhaird. When we got to Falcarragh, I think I had to crawl in the door.

The truth about me and golf, however, is that I could never hit a ball out of my way. Two stitches above my left eye as a result of standing too close to my brother, John, as we were practising hitting potato skins across the garden wall with a number two iron put an end to it. That, and a Cork management trainee, a graduate, who came into the company where I had my first job as a junior draughtsman. He wasn't three months there until he knew the names and the birthdays not just of the Works Manager and the Works Engineer, but of their wives and their children; and which Golf Clubs they were members of. The only way to succeed in business, he declared, was to somehow become a member of one or other of the Golf Clubs, preferably the Works Engineer's. He put me off golf forever. He was right though in picking the Works Engineer, who went on to become a distinguished Managing Director of the Company.

I didn't really see my wife being drawn into golf in those debt-ridden, high interest rate middle years of our thirty-five year marriage, or appreciate the depth of her need for a circle of friends where we were then settling in West Donegal. By the time I did, it was too late. The realisation that I had become second, or even third choice, after my wife's golf or her golfing friends, pushed me over an edge. I'm still there. I was ever a bad loser. In this, I suppose, I am like most golfers.

Chapter Two - Heroes

We grew up in an age of heroes. When, as youngsters, we played at racing, we tore around the place and either held our hands out in front of us, as if holding an unseen leather-bound steering wheel - in our imagination, we were the very cars themselves - or extended our arms sideways, dipping and raising them in turn as we weaved from side to side - we were now aeroplanes - and we shrieked out: "Charlie Manders". I don't suppose any of us ever really knew who Charlie Manders was. Some local speed ace. One story had it that he arrived to tea to some house in the Burnaby, that Liam Maguire's mother worked in, on his motorbike one afternoon, to find the two swings of the wooden gate unexpectedly closed against him. Without hesitation, he was said to have raced through it, smashing and scattering the two halves of the gate. Only after the tea did he apologise and arrange for the gate to be repaired.

One day, an aeroplane buzzed the town and snarled its way over "Rockport" and the top of the boat slip, then away northwards over the back of the pier. It wasn't one of the three Irish Airforce planes- we knew them by the Irish tricolour painted on the underside of the wings, and we had seen them on practice sorties before - so it too became "Charlie Manders".

I suppose our greatest hero of that time was Joe Louis. The Brown Bomber. Undisputed Heavyweight Champion of the World. He was magnificent. He hit so frequently and so fast that they had to use slow-motion cinematography to even count the blows. He crushed Max Schmelling and destroyed Primo Carnera, the giant Italian. Tami Mauriello he annihilated in the first round, reportedly angered by a sneak early blow. We, of course, didn't really get to see any of this until the new "Ormonde Cinema" opened about 1948 and we could watch the highlights of the fights on the newsreels, and go later to the special films that would be released afterwards. The term "black American" hadn't then been invented, and many of his own people condemned his acceptance, however limited or qualified, by the white community as tokenism and a betrayal, but for my money, there could be no prejudice after him. His career ended sadly, battered physically inside the ring and financially outside of it, but the image that lives is of that superbly fit, lithe, lean, beautiful body; head, shoulders and gloves thrust slightly forward in "attack mode"; in a photograph taken some time in the thirties.

I was born in the thirties, in 1937, the third of three boys, with two years between each of us, and my sister Kathleen was born in 1939. It inevitably followed then that, as soon as I got mobile, I trailed around after my two older brothers, Billy and John. The few photographs from that time show me as a sturdy, chubby little fellow with a distinct pout, and that, I'm sure, is the reason I was teased and taunted as "baby". I never lacked temper. Micheál Canning, whom I met on the first "Skipper Training Course", and who is dead these fifteen years or more, said years later: "Jesus, Hayden, when you lose your temper the fire comes out of your eyes."

As an infant, I was called both "Hitler" and "Spitfire", and that's how, perversely, Hitler became a sort of anti-hero to me. I can remember going to my first "Fancy Dress Ball" in a brown-shirt uniform, with a swastika armband and jackboots; all hired out of Gings, the costumiers - I was probably only fourteen - and I could not comprehend why my mother said: "Oh, no, Jimmy." But she blackened my fair hair and brushed a Hitler-style parting into it, and painted a black toothbrush-style moustache on my upper lip, and let me discover my own destiny.

Greystones at that time was the most Protestant town in the twenty-six Counties; the population was about half-and-half Catholic and non-Catholic. We grew up and it mattered little to us because we all had friends across this divide. But it was notable even to us youngsters that there was a pro-German sentiment in a lot of the Catholics and, where others might sing:

9

"Blacktop made a shirt,
Hitler wore it,
Churchill tore it"

We reversed it to:
"Blacktop made a shirt,
Churchill wore it
Hitler tore it.
Whistle while you work".

Blacktop Kinsella was a granduncle of mine, a great hulk of a man who was reported to have rowed a twenty-foot oar in John Spurling's original "Colleen Bawn", a working skiff that failed to win only two races in the regattas of the day. One of Derek Paine's books of photographs shows the "Colleen Bawn" crewed by John Spurling, Bill Spurling, Jack Darcy, James Whiston and George Archer. In another of Derek's books it's clearly Blacktop on the midship oar. His given name was John Thomas. I can remember kneeling at Blacktop's wake in Kinsella's house in Blacklion, about 1946, my eyes just level with the rim of the coffin, and seeing this great nose protruding above the rim. He was buried in the old graveyard in Kilcoole in the next grave to his sister, Katherine, my grandmother McKenzie. She died in 1923, when my mother was only twelve years old. Afterwards - that is, after Blacktop's coffin had been buried and the grave filled in again - my grandfather showed me the informer's grave. The book, "Kathleen Mavourneen" has a great account of this death and burial, and the curse that never would grass grow over his traitor's heart. With all the scepticism of a true Scot - both his parents were of Scottish stock although they married in Manchester and my grandfather was born within sight of Aintree racecourse - he cleared the grave and seeded it with grass. So he told me that day at Thomas Kinsella's funeral. One patch, he said, failed to grow and he had no explanation for it.

By the time of his death, Blacktop had too become a legend, with the reputation that he could snap the twenty-foot oar at will.

There was a revival of interest locally in skiff racing in the late 1940s and I can remember a triumphant crew being carried up the beach in the borrowed white-painted skiff "St. Joseph". By 1951, a rowing club had been formed and a new skiff commissioned, to be built by John Spurling, and to be called "Colleen Bawn the Second." John Spurling was the real hero of the original "Colleen Bawn". He not only rowed in it, but he had built it, and the skiff had lost only two races. One of these failures had been a dead heat at Wicklow Regatta and, in the immediate row-off, the Greystones crews had triumphed by a distance. I have heard it variously recounted as anything from twenty lengths to forty lengths.

The second occasion that first "Colleen Bawn" was beaten was in a race against a skiff named the "Venture". This had also been built by John Spurling, reportedly to give the lie to the growing legend that the "Colleen Bawn" could not be beaten. These skiffs, you should remember, were all working skiffs. They fished, hobbled, carried gravel ballast to coastal trading schooners, even pilgrims across the upper lake at Glendalough to Kevin's Bed. But the second "Colleen Bawn" was not the equal of the original and failed miserably at her first outing.

Chapter Three - Heroes II

I was stroke oar in the first race of "Colleen Bawn the Second".
Aged only fourteen, I was the youngest of an under-sixteen minor
crew whose luck it was to man the oars for the skiff's very first
outing at Ringsend Regatta. Some of the crews against us that day
could manfully have rowed an under-eighteen race, but the real focus
of attention was the other new skiff that was also on its maiden
outing. The "St. Luke", commissioned by the Irish Glass Bottle
Company Rowing Club from a Ringsend boat builder named Smith,
was a beautiful craft, drawing her lines from an earlier Ringsend
skiff by the same builder, the "St. Patrick". It projected an image of
sleek precision, and won seven out of eight races that day. The home
crowd skint the bookies to such an extent that I don't think they ever
came back to a Ringsend Regatta again. We were crushed, and
although we pulled our physical best for the rest of the season, our
hearts weren't in it. The following winter, the committee decided to
get a new boat, eventually named the "Shamrock", to be built by
Smith of Ringsend.

No one felt the failure of the "Colleen Bawn the Second" more
deeply than John Spurling and, even as the new skiff, the
"Shamrock", was only being built, he set up a boat on the stocks for
himself. Sixteen foot long and transom-sterned, she was as
precision-built as a Ringsend skiff and was a pure racer. The next
year, he traded the boat to his brother, Bill, and built a second
sixteen-footer with a little more beam to it. The year after that again,
or the next, he built a third sixteen-footer, for Jimmy Smullen and
myself. He had promised my father that he would build a boat for
him sometime, to replace the fifty-year-old Scottish-built fourteen-
footer, the "Kathleen" that we had bought from the Tuckers. Forty-
eight pounds the new boat cost us - me and Jimmy Smullen. The
"Kathleen" had originally cost seven pounds five shillings, delivered

Dublin, and an extra five shillings took it by rail to Greystones. That was in 1902. I'm not sure who the original owner was, but I think it was Bert Curling who sold it to the Tuckers, and we got it after Willie Tucker died in 1939.

Jimmy Smullen and I named the new boat "Mac Lir", after the Celtic god of the sea, Manannan MacLir, and I don't believe John Spurling ever built a nicer boat for rowing. And she fished as well. I can recall going off one evening to haul a couple of trammel nets and being hailed from the South Beach by the Ahernes - their father owned the Palace Bar in Fleet Street - who were together with Breda Reynolds and a friend, Marie Kennedy. We came that night to shore with ten stone of plaice, eight people on board, and a three and a half stone British Anzani outboard motor astern.

On another occasion, Kevin Dillon and I were rowing pair-oared with the beautiful ten-foot six sweeps that I bought from the Hammond Lane Metal Co. - salvage goods - when we encountered Breda Reynold's younger brother, Seamus, who was off in Jimmy Lennox's fourteen-foot boat with Jimmy and a one and a half horse power British Seagull outboard motor. Challenged, we invited them to a race and said we would row rings around them. And we did just that. We circled them twice, Seagull engine notwithstanding. John Spurling built one more boat; an abler but heavier sixteen-footer for his own family's use, but to my mind he never built a finer craft than mine. Then again, I never rowed in the real "Colleen Bawn".

One of John's sons, Johnny-boy, was stroke oar in the senior crew of the "Shamrock", his cousin, Cecil Gilbert, being bow oar. The two centre oars, midship and beam, were rowed by Christy Whiston and Jimmy Redmond. The cox was Michael Whiston, but everybody called him "Beezie". In the five regattas in their first year rowing together, they were third, second, first, second, third and never in our lives did we experience more exciting rowing. We roared ourselves hoarse every race, and sang all the way home in the back of J.P. Traynor's lorry, even when we lost.

The next year, that same senior crew won every race bar one, and the same I think in the year after that. From then on, they won all before them. At some stage, Paddy Redmond had replaced Cecil Gilbert on bow oar, and maybe even for a while, Johnny-boy Spurling; I have some memory of Johnny having an accident on a motorcycle. Cecil and Johnny-boy were those kind of fellows who didn't look especially strong but had muscles of steel. Jimmy Redmond had the physique of a Hercules and could have stood-in for Johnny Weismuller in any of his Tarzan movies. Christy Whiston was just lean looking, and Michael, his brother, was small, cheery and a great sportsman. Christy and Michael were cousins of my mother, their mothers being sisters with the family name of Kinsella. Paddy Redmond was strong and determined and had been a close pal of my own when we were younger. And how we cheered them.

In the year of "An Tostal" it was decided to organise a special race on the Liffey, between the winners of two heats to be rowed respectively at Dun Laoghaire and Ringsend. The race was to start at Guinness's Wharf and finish at Burgh Quay, just as the Head of the Liffey races of sculls, fours and eights, that were more familiar to the general public, did. The Ringsend heat was won by the "Stella Maris" from the Stella Maris Rowing Club. The "Stella Maris" senior crew was the Greystones crew's great rival in the early and middle years of the 1950s. They trained seriously, were superbly fit and, rowing shorter oars than the Greystones crew, generally set a faster stroke than the Greystones men. The older "Stella Maris" had a low freeboard and a raked stem, and always looked to be a couple of feet shorter than the other skiffs which were a standard 25ft. length with a beam of approximately 6ft. They rowed two twelve-foot and two fourteen-foot oars. By contrast, the Greystones crew rowed two sixteen-footers and two fourteen-footers. The "Stella Maris" crew generally started at fifty-five strokes to the minute, then settled at the still very fast pace of forty-two to forty-five strokes per minute. The Greystones crew with larger oars usually settled to thirty-four to the minute, and spurted by hitting the oars harder rather than by lifting the stroke.

At some stage, the old "Stella" was replaced by a new "Stella Maris", also built by Smith of Ringsend, that was said to be a half-inch finer than the "Shamrock". Later again, Smith built a new "St. Patrick" and we had it as gospel that the differences between the "St. Luke" and the "Shamrock" and the "Stella Maris" and the new "St. Patrick" were, respectively, one-eighth, a half, and a quarter of an inch. Smith, I believe, reckoned the "St. Luke" the fastest of all the skiffs that he built. Nonetheless, it was the "Stella Maris" that the Greystones men were to face on the Liffey because, you see, it was the "Shamrock" that had won the Dun Laoghaire heat.

I got to thinking that the "Stella Maris" would have the advantage of us, because all they had to do was row up the river and practise over the course itself. Without saying anything to anyone, I travelled into the city and went down along the quays to where the Guinness ships berthed below Butt Bridge. In those days, the Guinness that was exported - whether to Liverpool or to Manchester or to Bristol - was all brought downstream in the famous Guinness steam-barges and it was one of the sights of the city to see them off-loading the barrels and half-barrels and hogsheads onto the cobbled quays virtually under the loop-line bridge. And if anyone, in my mind, were to know the run of the river, it would be a Guinness bargee. I don't now remember if it was the barge captain or the mate, or just one of the deckhands that I asked, but I hit gold. I had already checked the time of the tide for the evening of the final and I remember that it was to be rowed on the ebb. The bargee named out every bridge for me and told me how the stream speeded up where the channel deepened as the river curved into the south bank at Church Street Bridge and Winetavern Street Bridge on the ebb. When I boarded the train for home at Tara Street Station that evening I had already walked the entire river from Butt Bridge to Kingsbridge, and had paced and sketched every arch.

Beezie gave me a right look when I gave him the sketch and told him where I got the information from, and he tucked the piece of paper away into a pocket.

On the evening of the race itself, we unloaded the "Shamrock" at Ringsend and, leaving the crew to kit out, crossed to Sir John Rogerson's Quay on the Port & Docks ferry and set off at the trot to get to the start at Guinness's wharf, just level with the brewery yard. We barely made it ahead of the two skiffs, which had been rowed briskly up river. The last bridge they cleared upstream, and the first to be negotiated in the race itself, was the single-arch Watling Street Bridge at Usher's Island. Its fine cast-iron spans are dated 1858, from the St. Helen's, Lancashire, foundry of Robert Daglish Jnr., and it lay down stream about two hundred and twenty yards from the start. At the crack of the gun, eight oars dug into the water, and again and again, as both crews clawed frantically to build up speed. As I expected, the "Stella Maris", with the faster stroke, made it to Watling Street Bridge first and had even increased their advantage by the next bridge, Queen's Street Bridge, to head the Greystone's crew through the centre arch.

The great shout that had gone up from both sets of supporters at the start had built into a rising clamour of jubilance and counter-exhortation as we all ran downstream along the quays with them. I disremember whether it was at Church Street Bridge or Winetavern Street Bridge that Beezie let the "Shamrock" fall away to the south side of the river, but I can still see the "Stella Maris" entering the centre arch in the lead, and I know we had sprinted ahead and were there to roar when the "Shamrock" emerged from the side arch ahead of the "Stella". That was the end of it really, but we ran and jumped and shouted all the way to the glorious finish; the "Shamrock" leading the "Stella Maris" under Capel Street Bridge, where the navigable arches are all equal; then flashing under the airy span of the "Ha'penny Bridge" and through the centre arch - tunnel almost - of O'Connell's Bridge to the Irish Press office at Burgh Quay.

There were other great national heroes at that time; Harry Bradshaw, yet again vindicating his true reputation as world-class with his victory, together with Christy O'Connor, in the Canada Cup, after the disappointment of the infamous 'ball in the broken bottle' incident; John Joe Barry, the Ballinacurra Hare, the fastest miler in the world on grass and the first Irishman to be awarded an athletic scholarship to the United States; the Rackards and the excitement of the great Wexford hurlers, and the train loads of supporters that we cheered, and counted - on one occasion, I think, eleven trains - on their way to Croke Park.

But I treasure the memory of our own, those great Greystones oarsmen, more than all of them.

Chapter Four - The Ultimate Hero

When I read in "The Irish Skipper" in January or February of 1986 that Val Hinds had died in the islands of the Pacific, I immediately wrote to Arthur Reynolds whom I had known since just after he started the "Skipper" in 1964. I wrote: "Val Hinds was our local hero supreme. A superb swimmer, he had swum the two miles of open sea from the Cable Rock at Bray Head to the point of Greystones Pier, then surpassed it by swimming three miles to the Moulditch Buoy and a mile and half back to shore. All this, and he was also the first man to introduce 'Scotch feathers' to Ireland".

I went on to tell how, as a newly appointed fisheries officer in Tanzania in 1964, I was given charge of Tanga and Kilimanjaro regions after first participating in an exceptionally good "Swahili Orientation Programme." This gave me a great understanding of the country but, for the first three months, I wasn't sure that my own approach to the job was the right one. I had little knowledge of local fishing methods and concentrated instead on marketing and organisation. Then, one morning, I received a parcel from headquarters in Dar-es Salaam that clarified all: the file of safari and monthly reports from the original fisheries officer on the coast, one Val Hinds.

At a time when it was still Tanganyika and a British Protectorate, Val travelled the coast by mtumbwi and ngnalawa, by dhau and by mashua, and had recorded all with perception and insight. A notable feature of these safaris by sea was his use of a button accordion and ceili and old-time music to break the ice (a strange metaphor for that steaming place) with the Shirazi fishermen along the coast. He moved later to Aden, briefly, then to the Pacific Territories, and it was my great regret that I had never the opportunity of meeting him in all that time. "But I'll meet him some day in Fiddler's Green."

Incidentally, an mtumbwi was a long, shallow dug-out canoe that was mostly poled in the shallows. The ngalawa was the pride of the East African coast, a magnificent, deep, dug-out canoe that was sailed as a trimaran with planing boards port and starboard. I have seen one more than twenty-seven feet long, and all of five feet deep. Mostly, they were adzed from a single trunk, but tradition demanded that a new craft always be built with a piece from an older ngalawa, even if it meant gouging a piece out of a perfectly good trunk to do so. Their enemy was the teredo, a boring mollusc, and it was a familiar sight to see ngalawas hauled out of the water, sitting on two half-rounds of coconut logs on the beach with a fire of dried coconut fronds set underneath them. After firing, they would be smeared with an evil-smelling paste of rotted shark livers.

The Mashua was a transom-sterned carvel vessel that, I suspect, was modelled on the European longboats. The dhau, built in the same crude manner, of coarse planks set on to rough mangrove branch frames, was undoubtedly older in design. There was nothing crude about its sailing performance, however, even with its shallow draft, and the dhaus and their crews fished the reef-tops with a juya seine without hazard. I wonder if they still do?

My ultimate hero, however, was always my father. Maybe this was because he went off to the War when I was only about three, and I didn't have him again, other than for yearly, or maybe twice-yearly visits home, until 1946. I've always understood that he went to join the (British) Navy and was turned down because he was colour blind. Whether or not that was so, I don't care, I've just been glad all my life that he came back to us.

He was my hero also because, somewhere along the line, I learned that he had "run away" to sea at the age of sixteen, and had travelled the world; and it became an ambition of my own to do likewise. The funny thing is that, after a fashion, I did just that. And a son of mine after me.

19

I don't know the reason or circumstances of my father's going - mine was my inability to say to my mother that I wasn't fit to face repeating the maths, maths-physics and physics exams that I had failed in the first year at university; and my son James's going was, as he put it, to see if he could survive a year on his own -but the time of my father's going, round about 1920, probably camouflaged his real reason.

I don't suppose any of us ever really spends enough time getting to know our fathers. Our mothers generally are, or were, more available and our problem with them was of being almost too close. By the time our father came back from the war, our growing independence seemed to take us from where he was at. But, over the short few years between 1946 and 1957, when he and my mother had to move to England, to be followed later by Eileen, Barney, Declan and Auntie Eileen, I gathered information in scraps. Always by listening to conversations with strangers when I was away with my father on occasional football excursions. Or to conversations with friends while walking to whist drives. Years later, when I lived in Donegal, both in Falcarragh and in Ardara, and he came on holidays from England, I was too awkward in conversation to be able to draw out his memories and his feelings. But we were relaxed with one another and that was something both of us valued. In a sense, I was the bird to his St. Francis, each giving the other that special thing, love.

Fan Donohue, his aunt, who was also his Godmother, told me of meeting him coming down the brae from Delgany to Killincarrig crossroads with a little bit of a cardboard suitcase in his hand.

"Are you for off, then, Hayden", she asked.

"I'm off, Donohue" was all the answer she got.

She had understanding, this tiny aunt of his, and to the end a great liking for him. On another occasion, she told of him coming in one morning to the kitchen of the house at the butcher's stall. This was the family house. His mother asked him, chidingly, where he had been the previous night. Fan thought he had probably spent the night with his half-brother, Michael, who had married and was living in the cottage in the square. But all the answer - and satisfaction - my grandmother got was: "I don't know. I must have slept somewhere. There's hay on me."

Years later, my Uncle Bernie, my father's older and only full brother, told me of being sent to London to collect my father and take him home. Father had some how made his way there, having first got on a schooner sailing from Drogheda, and was lodging in with someone from home. At the time Bernie was telling me this, Euston Station had been modernised - changed in the process - and Bernie asked me if I remembered how it had been. How the "Irish Mail" was always pulled in on platform 12, and the Glasgow night sleeper on platform 13? And did I remember also, he asked, that the gents' toilets and washroom were down around the back of the Glasgow train? When I assured him I did - I was frequently short-taken and think I knew the location of almost every gents toilet there was - he told me how Jim, my father, gave him his case and asked him to go ahead up the train and get a couple of seats while he went for a slash. Down around the corner of the Glasgow train, however, my father waited just long enough to get Bernie's back turned, then took off along the Euston Road for King's Cross and a train out to Tilbury. Bernie copped on only just in time to get off the train but, by the time he had back-tracked to the old-timer my father had been lodging with, and sussed out that father had gone for Tilbury, it was too late. Bernie reached the dock sometime the following day, just in time to see Jim waving to him from the stern of a ship that was drawing away from the dock, bound out for Australia. Father was helping to pull in the mooring ropes.

It was sometime in the early fifties that I came across his Australian passport, and being curious enough to ask him about it, got another little bit of the story. He had signed on for the voyage - the full round trip - this being standard procedure, and had jumped ship in Australia. Later, when he decided to come home, he had to get some old timer to sign an affidavit that he had been brought into Australia, unregistered, as a baby, his date and place of birth being correctly recorded as 1904 in Delgany, Co. Wicklow. He had gone to Australia simply because a pal of his had emigrated there and had written asking him to come out. Whatever port father got ashore at was the opposite end of the continent to where his pal was at, but they succeeded in making contact by letter. Each then, independently, decided to go and meet the other and both traversed the continent - and never met up.

I don't know how long he stayed there, or what decided him to come home, or even if indeed he spent some years in the merchant navy, but my Aunt Lizzie told me that my mother was there to meet him when he finally arrived. Aunt Lizzie, who was my Godmother, was really my mother's aunt, and her Godmother also. In the years after my mother and father had to move to England, and long after her husband, Peter Tipper, was dead and buried, I used to visit Aunt Lizzie, and it was on one of these visits that she told me there were three local girls who had a "notion" of father, but that it was my mother who met him at the boat in Dun Laoghaire, and that's how she got him.

There were other occasions, as I said earlier, always in casual conversations, when he talked about things he had seen; the Indian Rope Trick; that other great magic trick from the Indian sub-continent, the plant that grows and blooms from seed in an instant; in Australia, the casting of the bones. He told of being treated for severe sunburn by one of the "black fellows" who squashed up a big white maggot - a wichiti grub? - and rubbed the oil all over him. The treatment worked. Jack Sweeney told me of working with him during the early part of World War II in a camp at Ballitore in Scotland - it's on the Dornoch side of the isthmus between the Dornoch and the Cromarty firths. I later applied for a job as manager of a prawn processing factory at the same place. The 'forties job was the building of an aerodrome. Father liked to go to work on a decent breakfast, but this wasn't always possible in wartime. The others in Father's squad would hold on in the dormitory hut until they saw Father coming out the door of the canteen hut with a plate in his hand and a cry of "Babyshite for breakfast again lads", as he threw the wartime powdered egg to the winds. They knew not to bother that morning either.

He died in the car, beside my youngest brother, Declan, while being driven to Birmingham Airport to come to Ashley's wedding. Ashley is my Brother John's son and was the first of Mother and Father's grandchildren to get married. Declan is sixteen years younger than I. I had visited my parents earlier that year on my way back from a fisheries exhibition in Copenhagen, and my mother had said Father was going to come over for a holiday in July. He was to stay with John Gunning, one of his best friends from both the Greystones Soccer Club and the rowing club, but that she didn't think he'd make it. He wasn't strong enough. When July came, he put it off until August so that he could make it to Ashley's wedding. In the event, he didn't make it; not quite.

Billy and Declan decided we should take him home to bury him, although Father had often said he wanted Mother and himself to be cremated. I think all of us felt Billy and Declan's decision was the right one. At the time he died, he had been just twenty-eight years in England, and had come back every year for his holidays.

On the evening we took his remains to the Church of the Holy Rosary in Greystones, we gathered into my brother John's house on the side of the Little Sugarloaf afterwards for a cup of tea and some sandwiches, and I took the opportunity to speak to Billy. I felt sure he would want to say something at the funeral and I asked him: "Let me say it."

I wanted to plant Father where he belonged; where no one could deny him. This is what I said:

"I want to thank you all for coming here today to join with my mother and our family in saying goodbye to Jim. In the simplicity of his life, it could be said he was the first among my mother's children. Now that the burden of her concern for him has been lifted, the love for her life-long companion remains.

"There are not many left who can remember it was his father who asked Peter LaTouche for the ground on which this beautiful church is built. In the example of his life, he left us great gifts of honesty, integrity and charity. He paid every man his due; he gave a full day's work every day; and I never knew him to refuse a shilling or a sixpence, or a few coppers even, to any poor man who asked him for it in the street. He loved all his old friends and he made a new friend of everyone that he met.

"The morning after he died, I woke early and lay there thinking. I had slept peacefully because I knew that he was at peace. I was thinking of the words of the Catechism - you see, it was in this beautiful church also that we were examined in our catechism before the Bishop - 'that we shall all meet together with the self same bodies which we had in this life'. And I could imagine my father being taken in to dinner by St. Peter, to the same piece of corned beef and cabbage that I had almost bought the day before - you see, he was going to come up to me in Donegal after Ashley's wedding - and I could see the little smile that would come on his face, and I could hear the words he would say without any intended profanity - Good Jaysus - and knew that the answer would come from the head of the table - 'Yes, Jim.'"

I finished by saying: "Also in his own words and, as near as I can manage it, in his own manner - Cheerio, old pal!"

Chapter Five - We Knew Who We Were

When I was eighteen or nineteen, I wrote a rather fanciful short piece for a local roneod magazine that was brought out in the town of Bray. It started: "I'm no Lepride", said Jago Hayden. "My people came out of England and Scotland and out of all Ireland and, if they were small itself, or dark, it was not the smallness or the darkness of the Little People."

I was Jimmy Hayden, better known by my nickname, Jago. We were the Haydens: Billy; John; myself; Kathleen. Our father was Jim Hayden and his father was the old "Boss" Hayden, who had the butcher's shop in Delgany. Our mother was Annie McKenzie and her father was John McKenzie, who had the shop next door to S. Ferns' Draper, beside the chapel in Greystones. Grandfather McKenzie was also known as "The Boss" McKenzie.

During the War, when my father was away in England, my mother helped my Grandfather in the shop and, because the shop was just in front of the Holy Faith Convent School - the shop was actually leased from the Convent - and because Kathleen had come along just over two years after myself, and, I suppose, because the Convent got headage for every pupil, I was sent to school at the age of two-and-a-half.

After the War, my second sister, Eileen, was born, then Barney and later Declan. Barney was born with Down's Syndrome and, initially, was not expected to last three months. Later, the accepted wisdom was that people with Down's Syndrome wouldn't make it much beyond thirty-four. At the time of writing, Barney has just celebrated his fiftieth birthday and looks good for at least another thirty years.

Our Grandmother McKenzie had died in 1923, when mother was not quite thirteen. We never knew her. She was Katherine Kinsella and had sisters named Winnie, Mary Ann and Elizabeth and brothers, Willie and John Thomas. Another brother, Michael, was killed in the first World War. All the sisters of course, were called Aunts and I, for one, grew up not really knowing whose aunts they were; not for years. Except that Aunt Lizzie was my Godmother and was also my mother's Godmother.

It was only us older ones, who were born before the War, that knew our Grandmother Hayden, who was even then an old lady. She was more commonly known as "The Granny Reilly", her maiden name, presumably because my Grandfather Hayden had married twice. Our father was the youngest of the second family and had an older brother and sister; Bernie and Eileen. His oldest half-brother was Will, whose wife Lena's maiden name was Taaffe; and his other half-brother's name was Michael.

Our Grandmother and Grandfather Hayden passed away in 1945, and "Blacktop" - Thomas Kinsella - about the same time. The granny and grandfather Hayden were buried in the new graveyard in Redford and "Blacktop" was buried in the old graveyard in Kilcoole, of which he had been a caretaker, alongside my Grandmother McKenzie, who had been his sister. We, that is Billy, John, Kathleen and myself, didn't need to ask who we were; we knew who we were. Apart from all these connections, we had other cousins and connections; Haydens, McKenzies, Donohues, Kinsellas, Mannweilers, Whistons and others we didn't even know of. But, for Eileen, Barney and Declan, it became a different proposition altogether. For them, the world rolled over in 1957.

When my father came back at the end of the War, he went to work for "The Gent" Fox, who had a butcher's shop on the Church Road, the main street of Greystones. "The Gent" was a decent enough man but, after the manner of the time, didn't pay very high wages. After a number of years, Father left him and went to work for George Roberts, who had bought the old family place; the butcher's shop in

Delgany. It had been auctioned on the 9th. of December in 1942, some years before my grandfather and grandmother died. In the meantime, Billy got a scholarship to secondary school in 1945, then John did the same in 1947 and myself likewise in 1948. Kathleen followed in 1950 or '51.

Billy, John and I went to Synge Street Christian Brothers' School, travelling in daily on the Harcourt Street line. Kathleen was sent to boarding school, to the Holy Faith Convent in Glasnevin. In the meantime, Eileen, then Barney and then Declan came along and, by this time, Billy and John had got scholarships to university. I sat the Leaving Certificate examination in 1953 and, although one of the three youngest in the final year, succeeded in coming unexpectedly either second or third in the class. But I was too young to qualify for university entrance and, hence, ineligible for a scholarship. That was the year my Grandfather McKenzie died.

I have no doubt but that the shop fed us, not only during the War but in all those years following on from it when we were at school. My mother worked in the shop and kept what books there were. My grandfather's routine started at 5.30 in the morning and didn't stop until he closed the shop at eight or nine o'clock in the evening. Time finally caught up with him. An operation in 1951 that was said to be for a double hernia that had been too long neglected, weakened him and, over the next couple of years, he just faded. My sister Eileen is in no doubt about what ailed him. It was cancer.

I was in hospital when he died. A severely in-growing toenail had turned pernicious and the operation was to remove the root of the nail. The funeral was on a Sunday and I was collected from hospital, taken out for the afternoon, and brought back again afterwards to the hospital. I cannot, therefore, vouch myself for what happened that evening, but my understanding of it has always been that the Reverend Mother came up from the Convent, knocked on the hall door and asked to see my mother in connection with the renewal of

28

the lease - then some three months overdue - and raising the rent. What was certainly true was that this Reverend Mother was newly appointed and had clearly undertaken to secure the renewal of the lease with an enhanced return for the convent. It was an ill start for my mother's ownership of the business and an inauspicious time for her to inherit it. And, as if it wasn't sufficient that the depression of that time, 1953 to 1957, was gutting the business for my mother, the Revenue Commissioners thought to levy a back-tax bill on my grandfather for the years 1946, 1947 and 1948. By the middle of 1957, the business was gone, sold out from under us, and my parents had to move to England. The sum realised for the stock and goodwill barely covered the tax levy which itself was later successfully challenged. By that time, however, whatever the sale had taken in was gone on expenses and fees. I was left minding the younger ones, Eileen, Barney and Declan, at home, together with Aunt Eileen.

I don't know that any of us could today remember exactly when Auntie Eileen came to live with us; she became such an integral part of all our lives. The Blackberry Lane from Delgany, by Stylebawn to the Willowgrove, was a favourite walk of hers and, I suppose, all of us were introduced to it by Auntie Eileen as soon as we could manage a mile or two. But my clearest early memory is of being lifted up onto the end of Kathleen's pram at the wee gate lodge at East Hall where Will and Lena lived, after the bottom of the pram had been filled with apples from the Miss Eccles' orchard. I was just over two-and-a-half years old. I think she must have come to us about 1946 or 1947, after her mother died and after "young" Eileen was born. When the family place in Delgany had been sold in 1942, our grandparents and Eileen had moved into a beautiful thatched cottage near Killnacarrig crossroads, then later, when new Council houses were built just across the road from the Cherry Orchard, Eileen was allocated number three. Later still, I suppose about the time the old Boss Hayden and our Grandmother died, Bernie and May and our cousins Louise, Brian, Dermot and Brendan, moved out from Drimnagh to live there also. There was one later addition to the family; our cousin Alan.

This was the Aunt then, this Auntie Eileen, who minded young Eileen and Barney and Declan in 1957, while I was only one year in my first real job, with the Irish Glass Bottle Company, in a bungalow that was rented from the man, Bobby Mooney, who had bought our Mother's business. Billy and John were already married. Kathleen had just finished one year as a Junior Assistant Mistress, teaching in a school in Baltinglass in West Wicklow. I was on four pounds ten shillings a week. It's like a dream to me that the rent for the bungalow, in respect of which I was signed up as guarantor to my Mother, was three pounds a week. We survived from July until November, even though in the middle of it all, I had an attack of principles and left the Bottle Company because, for four pounds ten shillings, I was expected not only to have drawing skills but also to be able to cut out and file to shape - to tolerances of one thou. - sheet steel gauges for mould making. The time-served fitters on eight or nine pounds a week could not do it accurately enough.

The crunch came just at the end of November. Mother went in to hospital and was fretting for the kids. John, who at that time was living in England, got a message to me to get the kids over right away. That was on a Thursday evening. On Sunday morning, we pulled into Euston Station, three hours late; Auntie Eileen, young Eileen, Barney and Declan, who was not yet quite four years old - not for one more week - and my self, with half a ton of luggage packed into seven tea-chests. What paid the fares was a shilling-a-week insurance policy that Mother had taken out on my life and that had just matured with a value of forty pounds.

No scale could measure the pain of that year. Mother folded hers about with work and covered it with the joy of being re-united with her family again. Father never spoke of it but came back every year on holidays. Aunt Eileen swamped hers with the love she poured out on those who might almost be termed her surrogate children. She lived into her ninety-fourth year and was Auntie Eileen to a hundred nieces and nephews and grand-nieces and grand-nephews and great-grand-nieces and great-grand-nephews.

Barney's pain and mine were similar in character and remained buried within; his because of his handicap; mine because I have never been able to rip the thorns out of my soul. Eileen's and Declan's I have no idea of, but I know it was they who felt the need to ask Mother and Father and Auntie Eileen who we were. Along the way, they involved Billy in researching the family tree and set him off on a voyage of discovery. It's time for him to write the account of that journey. The rest of us are impatient for it.

Chapter Six - A Tunnel of History?

"I saw the chief of things that are gone,
A stag with head held high, a doe and a fawn"

I only once walked the long tunnel at Bray Head. More truthfully, was walked through it. The Blacklion Gang had set off to collect gulls' eggs on the cliffs at Bray Head and had started by making their way across the fields, working their way gradually in the direction of Ennis's Lane. And, instead of following the lane down to the "Gap Bridge" to pick up the cliff walk, which followed the line of the old railway, they walked up the tracks to the mouth of the tunnel. The Blacklion Gang wasn't really a gang in the organised sense of the word, merely an accumulation of lads from St. Brigid's Terrace, their ages ranging from ten to sixteen or seventeen, with a few other fellows thrown in. Most days, their spare time would be spent gathering sticks, not just for kindling but for fuel, or off with dogs hunting rabbits. A few of the older ones were very knowledgeable about the local birdlife and had great collections of birds' eggs. I happened to be with them this particular day.

The big tunnel at Bray Head is about three-quarters of a mile long and traces a slow S-bend from one end to the other. Somewhere, close to halfway, there is a wide ventilation shaft, which was driven down through the rock from the hillside above, and is topped with a great brick" chimney". Looking in to the tunnel from either end, one can see only darkness. Walk in to it, and after two or three hundred yards, you are in total blackness. This is what I was hauled in to, kicking and screaming. I was afraid of the dark; terrified of what might happen if a train came along. I think the two fellows holding on to me were Dessie Murphy and Kevin" Nipper" Glynn. We walked on the railway sleepers. For a grown teenager, a man, this makes for a short stride. For me, aged about eleven, it was a long one. The more we got into the tunnel, the wetter the sleepers became with the constant drip from the roof and, the more I slipped. And the more the two lads tried to stop me slipping into the gaps between the sleepers, the more they themselves stumbled. It's a wonder no one broke a leg.

The tunnel is quite an apt metaphor for my life and times, even more so for the entire century. I'm almost at the end of the tunnel. Were I to look back, I would see only the darkness. But I don't need to look back; I was already there. I saw the past. My children have raced away ahead of me. They have youth and have reached the start of the second tunnel. Through it, they already see the future, while I only know that it is there. But, if I don't tell them about the past, how can they know what it was like?

My earliest memory of Dublin is of crossing Butt Bridge with my mother while the train we had just got off at Tara St. Station puffed its way across the overhead Loop Line Bridge on its way to Amiens Street. Just ahead of us, drawing up the north quays past the Customs House, was a steam driven coal lorry. A second steamer rattled its way across the cobbles to Brooks Thomas's yard. That was where the Irish Life Complex on Lower Abbey Street now stands. The iron wheels of both lorries were shod with solid rubber tyres. I think there were a couple of schooners alongside the quays, but my memory may be playing mind-tricks, transposing pictures of masted vessels at the Customs House from an earlier age onto the reality of what I saw. I suppose I was about six years old.

There were other trips to Dublin, sometimes by train, other times on the No. 84 bus, a thirty-two seater single-decker that would crawl its way up Windgates, often grossly overloaded, before making its way through Bray, Shankill, Cabinteely, Cornelscourt, Foxrock, Stillorgan, Donnybrook and Ballsbridge and on via Westland Row and Pearse Street to the final stop in D'Olier Street. On those days, it was my delight to get my toes between the pillars of the balustrade of O'Connell's Bridge, to gain a little extra height, and wait for the Guinness barges coming up the river. These barges had either one or two deep holds forward of the engine room, which was right aft. What little cabin or wheelhouse there was sat on top of the engine room and was topped off with a fine tall funnel that had to be tilted back every time they went under a bridge.

This, together with the limited clearance of the bridge itself, caused a great spreading billow of warm smoke and steam and, like any other urchin, I gloried in sticking my face into it.

These earliest recollections of mine of Dublin are of a grimy, grey city that was, nevertheless, full of noise and bustle and people and excitement. There were trams with their clattering iron wheels and the grinding whine of their electric motors. Overhead, the power pick-ups hissed along the electrified wires and sparked at the junction points. There were some buses and lorries, and a few cars, but the hard clop of hooves and the harsh clatter of iron-rimmed cart wheels hit the ear more than did the murmuring noise of rubber-tyred wheels. About the docks, which at that time were active right up to the Loop Line, it was even busier and noisier. There, the Guinness barges unloaded their cargoes of full barrels onto the quayside where they were stacked, ready for loading onto vessels bound for Liverpool, Manchester and Bristol. There were barrels and half barrels and even, I think, quarter barrels. The slings could take two barrels at a time, or four half-barrels. As soon as the deck man had clipped the barrel-hooks over the rims of the casks, the winch-man pushed his steam-lever and, with a sudden wheezy whizzing clatter, the load would rise swiftly out of the hold and be swung in over the quayside. Occasionally, a hogshead, the greatest barrel of all, might need to be lifted and the steam winch would puff and wheeze more slowly as it strained under the extra load. Further down the quays at the transit sheds and warehouses, gangs of men wrestled heavy loads onto peculiar flat barrows that had a single small, iron-rimmed wheel front and rear and two larger wheels on one axle amidships. They could, therefore, be steered by rocking the load on the centre wheels; and roughly-dressed dock labourers pushed them into the dockside sheds or across the cobbled road into warehouse yards. This was a part of the city I was to become familiar with in later years; at first in my early teens when I came on errands to Eckfords ships chandlers, for longline twines and hooks, or ropes and catechu; later when I got into fishing properly and went trawling. Catechu was also known as 'barks'. This would be boiled up in a great vat of water in which our cotton nets and lines were steeped as a preservative, and its distinctive smell gave instant character to all ships chandleries.

There were other things that have stayed in my memory from those early visits to Dublin; the pillboxes at the top of Pearse Street, one set into the perimeter wall of Trinity College, and the other abutting the police station; and a stark line of bomb shelters down the centre of O'Connell Street. Either my mother or my grandfather took me into one of these to show me what it was. I remember their demolition also, and the noise of the compressors and the pneumatic drills as they tore the (minimally) reinforced concrete asunder. The noise frightened me even then, as it had on an earlier occasion when I was pushed in a wheelchair under the railway arch near the harbour in Greystones in the early years of the war, as Army engineers drilled charge holes into the stonework - in case we were invaded.

At the end of the war, two new motor vessels, the "Cambria" and the "Hibernia", were introduced by British Railways on the Dun Laoghaire - Holyhead crossing. These "Mailboats" - they carried the preface RMS - were beautiful craft and were quite justifiably regarded as miniature liners. An older vessel, the" Princess Maud", was also used on the run at peak times or, in later years, when either the "Cambria" or the "Hibernia" were out of service for refits or overhaul. The "Princess Maud", which originally came into service in the late thirties, was faster than the new mailboats and was dreaded by the country passengers because they got seasick more easily on her. My father had travelled on the "Maud" during the war, crossing on the Larne-Stranraer route, when the ship zig-zagged at high speed across the North Channel for fear of U-boats. I've heard him tell of standing watch with the lookout on the bow, even in wintertime, not only because he figured any torpedo would strike the vessel amidships or astern, but because the other passengers would get seasick and throw up without warning. I travelled on her a couple of times myself in the nineteen-fifties. The thing about the "Princess Maud" was that she was powered by steam turbine.

The first successful steam turbine was invented by Charles Parsons, the youngest son of the third Earl of Rosse, in 1894. It was the third Earl, William Parsons, who had built the great telescope at Birr Castle in 1845. Half a century later, Charles' steam turbine was demonstrated in a devastating manner to the Admiralty when Queen Victoria was reviewing the British fleet off Spithead on the occasion of her Diamond Jubilee in 1897. A specially designed vessel, the 110ft. "Turbina", powered by a steam turbine driving twin screw propellors, achieved 34.5 knots and made figure-of-eights around the two fastest destroyers in the fleet. Notwithstanding the enormous success of this Irish invention and its universal application - driving even the generators of atomic power stations - its clear that I lived through the end of the age of steam.

When I was fishing later on, I worked three months on the Scottish fisheries research vessel, "Scotia", and another four months on the fisheries protection vessel, "Longa". Both were steam-powered and had been built originally as T-class trawlers in World War II for escort duties accompanying 12-knot convoys to Murmansk. The"Scotia" had been converted to oil burning, but the "Longa" was still a coal-burner when I was on her, and every trip included a full day "coaling-up" and two or three days, subsequently, scrubbing the decks and washing down. The funny thing is, I cannot now remember anything "steam" about the trawl winches on the "Scotia', only that the dog-clutches were easy to engage; but I can still see myself on the stern of the "Longa" with an old Orkney man, named Willie Leslie, using a steam capstan to tighten up the stern lines when we moored alongside. Maybe it's because it was midwinter when I was on the "Longa". The steam condensed into white visibility in the cold air and we warmed our hands in it. Later still, I worked out of Middlesborough as mate on an Irish-registered vessel, the "Clearwater", which was on a seismic survey charter, searching for oil in the North Sea. The year was 1964. Just at that time, the last mine in the Cleveland Hills, which were to the south of Middlesborough, closed down after three hundred years.

The Cleveland Hills had been discovered to have deposits both of coal and iron ore and, what with the proximity of the river Tees, which provided both cooling water and a deepwater port in the estuary, this led to Middlesborough becoming an important development centre in the industrial revolution. Travelling to it by rail, I found I had to change trains at Darlington, where Stevenson built his famous locomotive, the "Rocket". As a boy, I had been given a book of "Great Engineering Marvels" and these included the "Transporter" bridge at Middlesborough and the lift-bridge at Stockton-on-Tees. Both bridges had been built to cope with the same problem - how to get ocean-going windjammers up-river to the wharves of Middlesborough and Stockton. The windjammers would be towed on this last leg of their journey by steam tugs. Is it any wonder I feel that if my children looked back through my eyes, they would be looking back through a tunnel of history? Were they to scan further, they would see the previous two and a half thousand years of the development of the ironsmith' s craft. Did I read even that early ancestors smelted iron in Africa one and a half million years ago?

Chapter Seven - Sea, Sand and Circuses

The news reports of our "famous" beef tribunal inspired me at the time to write a couple of verses and send them to The Irish Times for publication. This they did not appear to do. What had fascinated me particularly about the tribunal was the semantic agility of the lawyers who acted for every shade and sector of public and private interest, and the prima-donna prices they charged for so doing. Then, when the witness given seemed to indicate a proliferation of multi-limbed animals in our beef factories, I could restrain myself no longer. I wrote:

> *"We marvelled at John Duffy's greys*
> *And the Fossett's agility;*
> *And thronged, with sweaty pennies clutched*
> *The five-legged calf to see.*
>
> *But nimbler far are the circus stars*
> *That play the Castle Square;*
> *Just think of the millions of pounds it cost*
> *To discover the nine-legged steer. "*

John Duffy's team of eight dapple grey horses, all beautifully matched, were a famous circus turn in that period during World War II and ten or twelve years afterwards, when John and James Duffy's Circus was at its greatest. The mares were finely groomed and presented proudly and entered the ring at a canter to the music of the 'March of the Gladiators' or the 'Redetski March' or some similarly famous piece. If Patsy Greene were still with us, he could name it. Better still he would play it, because he did the circus circuit with his band sometime in the fifties or sixties. The Duffy's greys could have performed the act on their own - to the music that is. They entered the ring at a soft canter - 'bog-sodar' it would be called in Irish - numbered one to eight, and did a couple of circuits of the ring. Mr John Duffy a short stocky man in an immaculately pressed dress suit stood in the centre of the ring and cracked a long whip just to create an effect. Now I think it was Mr. John, and that it was Mr James that took the role of ringmaster. But I was only a child, and it was a long time ago, and if I mix them up now, small wonder for they were like twins. In the act with the grey mares there would be a pause, and the mares were then mixed up, the music would start again and in the space of a round and a half of the ring the mares would each find her proper place. We came to know the routine ourselves, almost as well as the mares, yet we always applauded wildly. Was it because of some sub-conscious yearning for a certainty that deep down even as children we feared we would never achieve in our lives? I wonder.

Fossetts circus had Bobby and Teddy Fossett. The younger Duffys performed daring and skilful equestrian acts, and were tightly disciplined; indeed it seemed as if Duffys Circus as a whole worked much harder to project a sense of 'style'. But they did not match the two Fossett brothers for the air of casual daring with which they performed their equally skilful bareback riding acts. The two circuses differed in other ways also.

In 1946 Duffys were the first to come to Greystones that year. We had moved for the summer to the little two- roomed cottage in the 'Bawn' that we rented every summer from Mrs George Archer, while we sub-let the house in Blacklion to families from Dublin. The 'Bawn' was on the harbour side of the railway arch while the circus field, which was also owned by Mrs Archer, was on the other. One thing you could be sure of was that on whatever day a circus was due, we were awake and there to meet it no matter how early it arrived. That year Duffys came with six brand new Chevrolet lorries with American army stars still painted on them. What stories we told ourselves about how well-got the Duffys were. When, later, Fossetts circus came, they arrived with one hundred and fifty one horses, mares, foals and ponies; mostly skewbalds.

They're the kind that would be described in Western novels as 'paints'. I can never watch a 'period' drama on television with immaculate carriages, groomed horses, and clean-gravelled roads without smiling to myself. I know what one hundred and fiftyone horses, mares, and ponies look and smell like, and leave behind.

The 'Bawn' was our summer home, I suppose, for the better part of twelve or thirteen years. I can remember Barney there, but not Declan. It was a row of some ten cottages built in pairs in a cul-de-sac on the sea side of the railway. They were basically two-roomed, but most had two extra rooms built on as lean-tos at the back. They had no running water, and only dry toilets outside at an ash pit. At their rere lay the railway embankment and the lane leading both to the dump and the cliff walk. They faced a high concrete wall that screened off the two storey houses on the North beach. I suppose the wall was really screening the 'Bawn' off from the better class properties to the front. Water had to be drawn from the pump that was just in off the main road, down around the corner of old Mrs Lynch's. Her cottage was no. 1, we were in number 2, and George and Mrs Archer lived in number 3.

At the other side of the big wall immediately in front of us were the Paines and the Thompsons. I think it was the Paines who were in the big house, which was the first past the old boat-house, then a cafe, at the North beach, and the Thompsons lived in a smaller cottage to the rere. Many properties in Greystones were like this, as many houses were let as a superior class of summer home. This is where Derek Paine grew up, the same Derek Paine who has published four collections of old photographs of Greystones. In one of his collections is a photograph taken from the vicinity of the boatslip, looking across the beach towards the boat-house, with the Paines house almost centre picture. A favourite view for many photographers, this one was published as a postcard captioned 'NORTH BEACH, GREYSTONES'. In Derek Paines book it is titled 'Sandy beach with children making sandcastles, 1940'. I well remember it; I was on the beach that day. I have never forgotten the extent of the garden that the children sitting next to us had created, pushing the sand up between their hands to make wee walls, as we all did, except they had made what seemed to us then to be an immense enclosure. Someone else came later and made a whole mini-estate of bucket-and-spade sandcastles. The photographer himself? What intrigues me is whether Derek's younger sister Joan was also on the beach that same day. Joan had polio when very young, and had to wear a leg-brace on one leg. Her parents were clearly either well advised or wise in themselves, because she was taught to swim from a very early age. And my first image of her being taken into the water was at the very spot to one side of those sandcastles. The woman sitting to one side of the 'gardens' in the photograph could easily be my own mother - the actual image is tiny, yet has the 'look' of her - but Mrs Paine and my mother were similar in build and height, and had the same breadth of face. It may be however that I am mixing days together in my memory, we spent so many at that spot. It was scarcely fifteen yards from there that I was nearly drowned for the first time, and no more than another twenty yards to the outer steps of the dock where I came close to drowning for a second time. All before I was seven years old.

It was from launching points on the rocks at the edge of the nearby boatslip that many of us learned how to swim. We would pick a spot where the water was just over our depth, then jump in towards the shore, arms flailing and legs kicking and hope to get inside our depth before we sank. It's a wonder any of us became good swimmers, but some did. I was more a dog-paddler than a flailer, and although I had, when small, delighted in crawling on all fours along the bottom with my head underwater, I hated splashing and being splashed and have been only a moderate swimmer all my life. The farthest I've ever managed was just a couple of years ago on holiday at the bay of Alcudia in Mallorca where I swam half a mile one morning with a combination of breast stroke and backstroke and felt very pleased with myself. Back then in Greystones my swimming progressed until I started doing little crouching dives and attempting short underwater swims from the bottom of the slip at half-tide. I got blinding headaches across the top of my forehead that put me off swimming underwater, or diving, for good.

It's interesting now to look back on who learned to swim where, and where they went next. The Blacklion fellows and the fellows from about the town generally tended to start at the slip, although the lads from the barracks - an old coastguard station - who were virtually all Guard's sons, swam also at the cove. Most of the 'pier' gang would have learned to swim either on the South Beach or that wee sandy beach at the harbour, and then moved on to the pier. The Blacklion lads, and others like Joe, Seamie, Brendan and John Sweeney from Arch Villas would also have swum from the broken-down North Wall, where at low tide you could pick your way across the shingle to find sandy bottom. The lads from lower Windgates were either farmers' lads, or worked on farms, and tended to come in the evening to bathe at the North Wall if the tide was right. Those from Delgany, or the Killincarrig side, would go to the South beach, which was nearer. Were you to add in the rather upper-crust families from the Burnaby estate, and to consider the entire demographic and religious mix that ultimately congregated about Greystones harbour, you could have busied a whole troop of sociologists for a decade.

Only two people drowned in Greystones in my time. One was a young handicapped boy named Meldrick, whose family was living in Rockport, one of the two houses just across the road from the top of the slip. I believe he was a spastic. He was playing hide-and-seek with his brothers on the rocks at the back of the flag-staff, and is thought to have clambered down the rocks and was unable to climb back. And he hadn't voice enough to cry out. An angler hooked his body the next day, but the line broke. I can still remember my father that afternoon in Bill 'the Munger' Doyle's boat hauling the mite's crouched wee body with the grapple and lifting him in over the side.

The other was a young boy, Herbert Tucker, who was left ashore when his parents went for a row in a boat, It seems he didn't want to go. It seems also that he fell off the back wall of the pier, unseen and unheard. His body was later found, standing as it were, on the deep ledge that shows only at exceptionally low spring tides. No wonder our Mothers barred the pier to us.

Later, after I had left Greystones, John Sweeney, who was a good swimmer, was one of two whose dinghy capsized one foggy night near the end of the North Wall. John saved his friend by draping him over the upturned dinghy, then was put astray by other voices, friends, unwitting contributors to the confusion who had by then clambered out along the North Wall, saying somebody was still missing. It was John himself who was lost in the darkness.

There were other circuses; Recos Brothers, which my mother said had been a great circus before the war; Jeserich Circus which was the first at which we saw the 'flying trapeze'; and even a Northern Ireland circus, Samsons. We had hours, days, and weeks of play and pleasure in the sand. And I was the lucky one. Some man went into the sea after me when I slid into the water at high tide from the rocks at the edge of the slip while Leslie Spurling was fishing a hand-line for me. That was the first time. On the second occasion I slipped on the green seaweed off the steps at the mouth of the dock, and a tightly buttoned overcoat floated me like a barrel while the wind blew me to shore. By the time I waterlogged and sank, the water was only waist deep. It's kind of right that I remember the others.

Chapter Eight - Keep Your Boat Off, Charlie!

"A woman
- has promised
- to buy me
- a sweep ticket"
The gaunt old man reached forward from his seat on the bollard and plucked my sleeve with a bony hand
"An' if I win"
The voice was a hoarse, half-shouted, whisper. "A punishment from God for all his cursing", our mothers told us
"An' if I win, Jemmy,"
His eyes lit up, and his face broke into a half-malicious grin.
"I'll sh--e on everyone in Greystones."

Then he laughed wheezily and his loose upper denture fell against the bottom with a click. The mouth closed and he sucked them back into place against the wheeze, showering us with spittle, and kept on laughing hoarsely through his teeth.

Poor, old, almost a grotesque; I later grew to be the same height as him. "Six feet" he would say; "the same height as Jesus Christ and Charlie Hemp": then his teeth would clack again. He was a man for all that; how could I ever forget him? The year he said this to us, to Sean Dillon and myself, was 1950 and I was off school recuperating from an appendix operation.

At the start of every summer Charlie Hempenstall would be about the slip painting up the two old rowing boats that he had, the 'Colleen Bawn' and the 'Dolly H'. The 'Colleen Bawn' he had bought from Desmond Daly, and I never knew who he got the 'Dolly H' from. He certainly was no seaman, and my father once said to me that he had probably trapped rabbits all over England and Ireland. But hiring the boats out, both to locals and to visitors, was his only way of earning a shilling. And the hoarseness - I am certain he lost his voice to a combination of diphtheria and scarlet fever; one of the great hazards of his lifetime. At this time every year also he would come out with a great spate of imagined adventures, that is if he had anyone to tell them to. That year Sean Dillon and I were around and he regaled us for three days with yarns of himself and Blacktop riding white horses across London's Westminster Bridge for a bet; of fighting both pygmies in Africa and fuzzy-wuzzies in the Sudan, and God knows what else. There was so much I've forgotten it all.

When the men who hired out rowing boats at the slip had 'tacks' that came ashore on the rising tide, they often preferred to get some young fellow to keep the boat off, or keep it afloat, rather than pull it all the way up the slip again. And we, as young fellows, would pester them to be allowed to do so. "Keep your boat off, Charlie?" was a common cry from us. Some years earlier, Charlie had another boat, a seven-foot punt made out of hardboard. It had been painted to give it some degree of waterproofing and while it lasted it was in great demand, especially from us younger ones. I can remember giving Charlie sixpence for a tack in it. Mind you it was rare for any of us to have a sixpence. That much would buy you two thrupenny bars of Cadburys chocolate, or would get you into the fourpennies in Hipples picture house and still leave enough for a tuppenny ice cream in Charlie Pennycook's. Mrs Pennycook was a sister of Mrs George Archer.

George was the patriarch of the harbour. He had been about boats and fish all his life, and if he hadn't got the height to be a biblical style patriarch, he had the breadth and the beard. A great black-brown beard, you would swear it had been dyed in the catechu we preserved the nets with. George had a rake of boats, the biggest of which was the 'Daisy Belle', a heavily built twenty-two or twenty three footer which he hired out to sea anglers on Sundays. The anglers were all Dublin men, a lot of them members of 'The Knights of the Silver Hook', who enjoyed the fishing but who really came to get the week's dinner for their families. The 'Daisy Belle' was so heavy that it couldn't easily be hauled up the slip if a storm blew up. She broke her mooring lines in the dock one particularly savage night and came to grief on the rock walls of the dock. George's other boats included a white eighteen footer, which was much admired, and a twelve-foot punt, as well as two or three fourteen footers - the handy size. When George died, my father hoped he might have a chance of getting the white eighteen-footer, but it went forty-two pounds at auction; more than ten times my father's wage packet.

I don't know where George's white boat came from originally, but both its bow and general lines were similar to Peter Byrne's fourteen foot 'Maureen', which was built in Athlone, and indeed to Jack Sweeney's fifteen/sixteen footer. The 'Gull' Field's and the 'Munger' Doyle's boats also looked as if they came from the same tradition of building. The 'Maureen' was perhaps the lightest boat of her size in the harbour, and was greatly in demand by the lads for keeping afloat. Peter had another boat, a sixteen footer, which didn't look that special but which had a surprising turn of speed when rowed pair-oared. This simply involved two people rowing, one oar apiece, each on a separate seat. (Thwart would be the correct nautical term, but we always called them seats.) In one of the handful of regattas, in which pair-oared races were organised as well as skiff races, I seem to remember coming in second in one of Peter Byrne's boats while his other one took the first prize; and the oarsmen were Lesley Spurling, Stanley Paine, my brother John and I. I can't remember who rowed with whom, but if the race had been another hundred and fifty yards longer we would have had them.

I don't suppose there was a nicer matched pair of boats in the harbour than the 'Connie' and the 'Lily', two fourteen footers. When I was small, I used to think they were George Archer's, but it was really Bill Spurling that owned them. He named them for the two Archer sisters, Connie and Lily. Bill was a house painter, and a very trim man. He prided himself on his nautical experience, and made much of the need for things to be made "shipshape and Bristol fashion".

He showed us splices and knots, none too complicated, and maintained we could only learn such things in the navy. We doubted he had ever been, but in hindsight he certainly challenged us, and we taught ourselves splices, and crown knots, and double crowns. Sean and Kevin Dillon went out and bought a book of 'Seven thousand knots and splices' and at the end of it could have rigged out a windjammer.

One of Bill's favourite knots was a 'Monkeys fist'; the one used at sea on the end of throwing lines, but he never did it in front of anyone. I figured it out one day and we all practised it like mad. There was a white boat on the slip, which was owned by Brian Burn, the son of a dentist who moved into the town. We thought it the same as a varnished mahogany boat that was earlier caretaken by George Archer, and that when the Burns got it they painted it white. But I have been assured I was mistaken. The white boat was bought from Horace B. Hammond who had a shop in Dublin selling marine items and outdoor equipment. Brian, though older than us was a silly kind of a young man, and had no experience of boats, or of the sea; certainly nothing that could compare with us salty dogs. So we presumptuously believed. He had however fastened a fine anchor-rope into the bow of the white boat; in fact he had someone splice it into the ring-bolt in the stem, with the other end spliced into the anchor. Thinking to play a trick on Brian, and to have it laid at Bill Spurling's door as it were, Sean Dillon and I unspliced Brian's rope - a three inch circumference cable - from the anchor, led it under a thwart and tied in it the biggest 'Monkeys fist' you ever saw. But they figured us out, as we had figured the knot out, and we restored all to rights a handful of days later.

That's the way our summers went. We played among ourselves, keeping boats afloat, building soft sugar- loaves of sand in the dock and jumping on them from the steps, occasionally being asked to row some visitors in a hired out boat, and getting paid for it. The visitors, and we ourselves, were watched out for by the men who were always at the slip. Our pals were anyone who was lucky enough to be clear of chores at home, and the likes of the Floods, or the Brindleys, the McKeevers or the Mulherns, Dublin families who took homes for the summer in Greystones. Occasionally they, or ones from the pier gang, would hire boats out and have mock-battles, splashing one another with the oars. At such times, we seized our opportunity and rowed in fast like pirates, true surface-raiders, to splash all parties, then hastily beat a retreat out to sea around the back of the pier. We had the advantage of them. We were brought up with wet britches. After all, when we were young we had goes on Charlie Hemp's hardboard punt. It lasted surprisingly well until a stone cracked a hole in it when it was being beached. The hardboard softened steadily and the hole grew bigger until, even with a handkerchief stuffed into the hole, held there, while someone else manned the oars, all that we could manage was one round of the harbour. Then we rowed like mad for the beach, half-sinking, ready to jump ashore as soon as the stem touched.

Charlie's 'Dolly H' wasn't much better. It was an old boat and leaky past being cured by the application of putty, or of being 'moored off' and sunk. Most of these rowing boats were built out of white deal, which split or 'rented' when the wood dried out. The usual, once-a-year cure for this was to 'sink' or semi-submerge the boat at the start of the summer. Then it would be anchored out in the harbour overnight.

'Mooring off' was just a convenient way of anchoring the boat, while still being able to haul it in from the shore. All the boats had three or four fathoms of a painter - a light rope - fastened into a ring-bolt in the bow. The end of this was hitched into the ring of the anchor, one tine of which was then balanced on the bow. Finally a shore-rope was secured with two half-hitches to the crown of the anchor, and all that was then necessary was a good kick or a shove to send the boat on its way out into the harbour. When it was far enough off, a sharp tug on the rope dropped the anchor. Remote control at its simplest.

Billy Kinsella and I, and I think Ronnie Tucker, rented out Charlie Hemp's 'Dolly H' one evening to go mackerel fishing. It was late enough, maybe after nine o'clock, and Charlie was reluctant to let it out, as he was just about ready to go home. And we hadn't got nearly enough money for him. I think the going rate for an hour was one shilling and eightpence, the price of twenty 'Players' or twenty 'Goldflakes', and we could only muster a shilling and maybe a penny threefarthings. I threw my leg over the little bicycle I had, and away like billyo to the 'Bawn' to see what I could get off my Mother. She gave me a sixpence, and for the princely sum of almost one shilling and eightpence, and the promise to pull the boat high up the slip when we got back, we had the 'Dolly H', and a good bailer, for the rest of the evening. Our own boat, the 'Kathleen' I should explain was already out after the mackerel. We got twenty-three mackerel that night, all on spinners, and I don't think I ever had more fun fishing. We rowed away north past the 'dipping tank' to the 'gap bridge', then away out to sea, then back into the 'burrow' and almost as far as the 'red rocks'. It must have been mid-summer because the light held, and when we saw the Bray-owned passenger launch 'Congress' outside us with spinning lines, we followed them out and right up into the 'Brandy Hole', beyond the 'Cable Rock'. It was nearer one than midnight by the time we got the 'Dolly H' safely pulled up the slip that night, and my mother was waiting for us at the entrance to the 'Bawn'; but little we bothered with anyone else's fears for our safety.

It was my father who had first taken us into the 'Brandy Hole'. This was a bit of a bay - in fact there were two bays, and no one appeared to be sure which was the right one - beyond the Cable Rock which was off the southernmost tip of Bray Head. This put it just beyond the farther end of the second tunnel. It couldn't be seen from either Greystones or Bray, and what with deep water close inshore was said to have been ideal for smuggling. Hence the name. In those years after the war my father liked to take us out rowing, and usually declared himself 'tired' to get us to take the oars. But on this occasion, a fine afternoon, he seemed to want to take us further, and although I can't be 100% sure, I think it was my sister Kathleen and Ronnie Tucker who were in the boat with us. There were two shingle beaches in the Brandy Hole, both backed by concrete ramparts reinforcing the rock below the railway line, and timing the wave just right, father took the boat ashore on one of them. I think it was the sight of the guillemots flying out of the drain holes in the concrete rampart that had got his curiosity up, and once ashore he climbed up and poked his arm into one hole after the other. That is, until a guillemot flew out and sh-t on him. Or so we thought, and him, and he said it. And we giggled the whole two and a half miles back to the harbour. By the time, years later, I found out that what guillemots do is 'spit' a noxious yellow oil at their disturbers, the 'brandy hole' had long since served its purpose as a name for a place that was beyond the horizon. A place from which one might glimpse the future?

Chapter Nine - 'Them's Only Daltys'

'Shoot, damn you, thems rogans'
'Hmmph, them's only daltys'

My Mother's cousin, Jim Kinsella, had a twenty-foot skiff called the 'Elsie'. It was the only registered fishing boat in the harbour and carried the numbers DI03. Some years later, when John Spurling built the 'Mac Lir' for Jimmy Smullen and I, we registered it as a fishing boat and were allocated D212 as a registration. The 'Elsie' was an old craft, dating I suppose from my grand-uncle Blacktop's time. It was always painted dark green without and tarred within, and as it was fished mostly for beach seining - draftnetting- it carried a considerable ballast of the coarse South Beach sand bound up in the tar in the well of the skiff. The 'Elsie' was also my real introduction to fishing.

I may have caught my first fish when I was only about two and a half, a mackerel on a spinner that when unhooked jumped up off the back seat of the 'Kathleen' and smacked me in the gob and left me bawling. I was still in short knitted woolly pants. Indeed the first lobster I ever caught was also taken in the 'Kathleen', about fifty or a hundred yards straight out from the point of the pier, when a little six inch lobster managed to get the tiny hook I was fishing in to his jaws. It can happen. Billy and John caught more than one lobster, fully grown, on the long-line. I had other experiences hand-lining in the 'Kathleen', the most extraordinary of which I always thought was a day I was detailed to row old Mister Johnston, Uncle Bernie's friend from Inchicore. We couldn't get bait to start with; the tide was in and so we couldn't dig lugworm. But Mr. Johnston sent John and myself off to gather snails from the crevices of the stone wall around the little field at the entrance to the Bawn. Our sister Kathleen might have helped us too. I'm sure also that was the time Mr. Johnston suggested to my mother that she could get rid of the big warts that were all over John's hands by letting the snails crawl all over them.

They disappeared within a week. However, I was the only one who went out with Mr. Johnston that day; and we only went as far as the 'Cove' - that was just in front of the 'Grand Hotel' - and we dropped the anchor and fished there for a couple of hours. We didn't get many bites - but we came back with a pound and a quarter, and a half-pound plaice, a mackerel and a three and a half-pound red gurnard, the biggest I had ever seen up to then.

Fishing with the 'Elsie' was different. To start with Jim Kinsella had a draft licence to fish salmon and trout. I think it was a drift and draft licence. The Fields - Mick who was commonly known as 'the Gull' and his brother Jim - had also a draft licence. These were the men who seined through-out the season, for seatrout, for mackerel, for pollock when they were running, and in years in which the fish lay inshore in September about the 'Swans Rock', even for codling. Fishing at night called for a different technique to that used in daylight. By day, the net was shot out from the shore in a semicircle, usually in great haste after fish had jumped adjacent to the boat. Then the seine was hauled from both ends onto the beach, the fish being gathered up in a deeper section in the centre of the net. This type of net was known as a seine net. The way it was pronounced locally, you would think it was a 'sine' net. At night, the net could be fished in the same manner but very quietly so as not to disturb the fish, which were lying along the shore at night. This was called 'loobing'. Years later Albert Swan, from Killybegs, who was the greatest fisherman in Ireland in his time, told me of standing on the shore of the sea of Gallilee and realising that the miraculous draught of fishes was taken just as the fish came off the shore in the morning. There was another nighttime technique used in Greystones, and this involved drifting a net along the shore, gradually allowing the outer end to fall in towards the beach until finally both ends were hauled ashore as normal. But with this net the bag, or deeper section, needed to be on the outer end of the net, and to fish this way for trout, you needed a drift and draft licence. There were those who had such licences, but if they had they kept quiet, because this was a very good way of fishing and they didn't want the rest of us to know about it. But I'm ahead of myself. All these ways of fishing needed a man on the shore to hold the rope or bridle from the end of the net. This was the 'swang', and a youngster of six or seven or eight was just perfect for any man to have, to sit on the gravelly beach and actually hold the rope while waiting for something to happen.

In a manner that can scarcely be appreciated today this was an innocent kind of pass-time. Men went to fish about half-past seven in the evening, after a day's work, and after their tea; or for those men who had no dinner in the middle of the day, after their evening meal. The crew of the 'Elsie' was usually made up of Jim and Jack Kinsella, James Whiston who was usually known only by any one of a pair of nicknames, and either Beezie (Michael) Whiston or my father. Tommy Redmond would already have walked down the railway line on the look out for fish jumping. If the intention was to go North to the 'Burrow', towards Bray Head, he would have walked up to the gap bridge, then along the beach to the rampart wall at the Burrow itself. More often then not, however, the 'Elsie' went south. The North Beach, the Gap Bridge and the Burrow tended to be the favourite of Mick and Jim Fields, and later of Joe Sweeney, and it was usually only when they scored with two or three stone of white-trout that Jim Kinsella went north.

Jim's preference was the beat between the culvert and the Three Trout river on the South Beach, or even further to the Money river or the 'piles' at the North end of the Kilcoole beach. This was despite the fact that the tides were stronger there, and more likely to he strewn with 'fasteners'. The wreck of the 'John Scott' for instance was off the telegraph pole with the four stays. The technique of dealing with fasteners was for the skipper, who was never called that, to take the boat out along the cork line, pulling the skiff along hand over hand once the seine net had been shot, until he reached the centre of the net. The other men, who would all have piled ashore as soon as the bow of the boat hit the beach, would by then be hauling the two ends of the net gradually onto the beach; one each on the back-rope - the cork line - at either end, and another two men hauling the lead-rope. Tommy Redmond, or even Jack Kinsella, would encourage the others "keep the leads down". If they felt that the lead-rope had come fast on a stone, they would call out "fast", and Jim would manoeuvre the skiff around until he found the fastener and then lift the netting until the lead-rope just cleared the stone, letting it fall immediately in case any fish might get out. For such a solid dependable man, he was terribly likely to get excited if there were fish in the net. It was said he once plunged over the side and wrapped his two arms around a fine twelve pound salmon caught in a bight of netting for fear it would get away, and the men on the shore had to haul like mad in case he drowned.

There were always stories, little events like that. My father once lost his pocket-watch over the side as he was lending a hand to shoot the net only to have it hauled ashore, still ticking when the net was taken in. It was a 'Smiths' pocket watch, and I believe it might have cost him all of five shillings during the war. It's funny, but after my parents had to move to England in 1957, he got a job in Smiths, just off the Watford by-pass.

One Summer, the mackerel shoals were particularly active, 'skulling' right up to the beach even in the middle of the day. Although it was summer, Jim Kinsella was away with the horse and dray delivering coal. This was his main business. It had been started by his father, Thomas, and my Grandfather McKenzie, at the time my grandfather first took on the lease of the shop from the convent. Jack however took time off from the golf, where he worked, to take the skiff out and assembled a very motley crew indeed. The oldest of them was Billy Kinsella, followed by John Whiston who was only a year or two older than I. Then there was myself, and I think perhaps Paddy Redmond. And although I don't remember him, I'm sure Tommy Redmond was already down the railway line ahead of us. The railway line ran right along the beach all the way to Wicklow.

Tommy Redmond had the eyes of a falcon, although we doubted him for years. Never, though, after the year in which a prolonged storm cleared a six-foot depth of sand off the whole of the South Beach. Nobody spotted the thousands of long-lost coins being uncovered as successfully as Tommy. He was thought to have gathered more than twenty pounds in five days. I think the next best was either Leslie or Johnny-boy Spurling, with four pounds and some odd shillings and pence. Tommy was known for other skills also. No one could match him at digging lugworm for longlining. He was one of the original foursome - it must have been during the war - that built Larry Ryan's hut, the finest fishing hut on the beach until Jim Kinsella built a new one about 1950. This same 'Larry Ryan's hut' was years later to be sawn in half when two of the successor partners fell out. Right down the middle. One other year, when Tommy Redmond had hurt his back and couldn't stoop, and when Osborne Spurling was long-lining, Tommy Redmond dug bait enough for both of them, way out on Merrion Strand where the biggest lugworms were to be found. Ozzy told me later he got a pain in his back just picking up the lug, so fast did they come. But I'm away from myself again; it's the year of all the mackerel I'm talking about.

That day, we rowed the skiff all the way beyond the piles to the Kilcoole beach, and although we saw mackerel skulling offshore, we didn't even get to make a shot. In the middle of the day, we hauled the skiff ashore and Jack shared his mutton sandwiches and a bottle of water with us. John Whiston and I had our swimsuits with us and we decided to take a dip. John was first in the water and swam parallel to the shoreline in waist deep water using the breast stroke. I was amazed at how good he was and ran along the beach keeping pace with him. 'Then he turned to swim back to the boat again, and we all burst out laughing to see him being swept backwards at a rate of knots towards Wicklow. We hadn't realised how much tide was in it, right up to the shore.

If we didn't get mackerel that day, we got pollock later that same year. I think it must have been in the month of August, during an extended spell of real foggy weather. Alternatively hot and cold, with banks of fog sweeping down the channel, then clearing at other times, the 'fog rockets' from the Kish light ship twelve or fifteen miles away, could be heard day and night. Shoals or skulls - schools, I suppose, is what was meant - of pollack started to appear, anything up to three or four hundred yards off. When they broke the surface, they did so aggressively, and the sound they made could be heard fully a quarter mile away. There had always been talk of 'Rogawns', some local name for big pollack that schooled so fast they could almost never be caught, and that could carry the net away, but I had never seen them. They were truly legendary, almost mythological.

At ordinary times, when the skiff was lying lightly at anchor just off the beach, with the oars pulled across the gunwales, the bow just rising and dipping in the swell of the waves, the stern crunching now and then in the coarse gravelly sand at the shore line, someone like myself sitting on the beach with the 'swang' either in my hand or tucked under my feet, the men motionless with their elbows across the oars, and Jim Kinsella like a veritable Peter astern of the net, the silence would now and then be punctuated by tales of occurrences from other times, other nights. Between these murmurs of conversation, little would be heard except the sssshh of waves along the shore and the plop of tiny pollack jumping and falling back into the sea again just off the shore where the bootlace weed grew. These I knew to be 'dalties'.

One evening, the story was told of another very foggy evening when they had decided to call it a night and head for home. By 'home', you might understand 'Danns', the harbour bar, because they usually managed to get ashore in time for a couple of pints before closing time. They rowed as usual along the shore, not exactly setting the straightest course in the world. The skiff tended to fall in towards the beach until the blades of the shore-side oars grated into the sand, then the offside oarsmen pulled more easily until the boat came off the beach again; and then the procedure repeated itself all over again. 'The evening of the bad fog they had rowed north along the beach, past the culvert, until they came to the 'Swans Rock' which was bare because it was low tide. There wasn't water enough to pass inside, as sometimes there might be, and they had to circle outside the rock to clear it. As they did this, the fog lifted enough for them to see the lights at 'St David's', the most easterly house on the seafront - the back of the rocks we called it. They decided to chance it across the open stretch of water, knowing they would feel silly if any man suggested tracking in to follow the shore. And as surely as they left the Swan's rock, just as surely the fog thickened in on them again. Each unwilling to admit their predicament, they rowed in total silence for an age, until they suddenly heard the heavy surge of waves washing over rocks, and in a panic threw out an anchor quickly, fearing they were about to be thrown on the rocks at Bray Head. They were scared but sheepish men by the time the fog lifted two and a half hours later and they anchored in the mouth of the harbour.

"Shoot, dammit, shoot; thems rogawns". I never saw anyone as excited as Tommy Redmond got that night as he ran down off his vantage point on the railway onto the beach. Up and down the beach that evening we went, the men in the boat rowing frantically, trying to anticipate where the pollack might school next along the shore, and Tommy Redmond and I running apace with them with the 'swang', splashing backwards and forwards across the outflow of the 'Three Trout' river. Eventually we made a desperate long-reaching shot, and hauled frantically to close the opening at the tail of the net even as the fish thrashed their way out the gap. We hauled forty boxes of three to fourpound fish; something like two ton, all in all. When they were loaded into the boat, they filled it completely up to the seat level, and only two men could stay aboard to row it back to the harbour. As we trudged our way back along the beach towards the lights of the town, Tommy Redmond was still repeating the refrain he started as the first fish started to come ashore. "Thems only dalties. Hmmph! Only dalties."

Chapter Ten - Cast Your Bread

The year John first went to England to work at the peas Billy was left
with no crewman for the long-lining. I was next in line and that's
really how I got into fishing.

My father had gone to England at the start of the war when I was two
and a half or three. I can still remember the night he went, because
he cleared three bags of papers out of the attic, and burnt them in a
bonfire on the path in the back garden. I had clamoured so much to
see what was in the loft up under the roof that he lifted me high over
his head up through the trap. I have a memory only of a dark place
of rafters and bracing timbers dimly lit by the light of a single candle.
I remember the bonfire though, which was set alight as a signal to
Jimmy Lot who was to go away with my father. The Lots lived half
a mile away in Crow Abbey. And I vaguely remember Connolly's
hackney car coming to the gate to take them to the mail-boat at Dun
Laoghaire. The bonfire of papers is still real to me over fifty years
later; I tramped through the ashes for days afterwards. It's funny, it's
only recently I have realised what was in those three sacks of papers.
The records of the butchers business that failed on my mother and
father after they got married in the thirties.

I never remembered Jimmy Lot coming back from the war, but my
father did, and even came at times during it. I have always
understood he went off to join the navy but was found to be colour-
blind. At any rate it seems he spent the major part of the war
working on the ground staff of an aerodrome near Silloth in
Cumberland, and stopped part of the time with a family named
Collins in Carlisle. When he came home on visits during the war, his
brown case, or the big leather valise that was his also, would have
tins of Tate and Lyle golden syrup, and tins of fruit or jam – things
just not available at home – buried deep under his clothes. But that
wasn't the only contraband. He invariably had hanks of cotton
twine. Long, evenly hanked and tightly wrapped in the manner of

the time, brown-barked, full one hundred fathom lengths of best cotton twine for long-lines. There were always the two sizes, a thicker one for the long-line back, and a thinner one, about twice the thickness of the jute shop-cord, for the snoods. We wouldn't have known at that time who the twine was for, we were too small, but I presume it was for Joe or Larry Ryan, or the Sweeney's, or perhaps for "Munger" Doyle who fished with his brother Thomas. The 'Munger', whose real name was Bill, baited his line into a shallow kind of an oval creel, with only a strung piece of twine separating the baited hooks from the heaped coils of the line itself. Everyone else used troughs.

I'm sure it was father, when he came home in 1946 after the end of the war, who encouraged Billy and John to make up a long-line of their own. We had our own boat, a fourteen foot clinker-built white deal rowing boat which had been built in Glasgow in 1902, and was one of a pair that had been shipped to Dublin for fourteen pounds ten shillings for the pair. I think ours was bought originally by Bert Curling, and was later sold after it had laid up in a shed for a long time to Willie Tucker. We bought it from the Tuckers in 1939 when Willie died of a brain haemorrage, and they were to have the use of it whenever they wanted it. We called it the "Kathleen". A Mister Johnston, who lived near our uncle Bernie in Inchicore and who was a keen angler, started coming out from the city for a day's fishing on odd Saturdays, and this led to me being detailed to take him out in the boat occasionally. Father used to take me out spinning for mackerel, and would say after a while that he was tired doing all the rowing and get me to take the oars. Two eight-foot oars are a handling when you are only nine or ten, and I was expected to feather the oars as well. Mr Johnston was a carpenter, and when Billy and John started long lining he made them a trough. It was a neat job, light but sturdy, and was finished with a narrow bit of a lath at the front, to stop any baited hooks falling off the tray. But it was flat-bottomed. The troughs made locally were much more shapely, with the bait-tray and the sides and the back of the trough sloped and canted to keep the baited hooks snug against one another and to make more room for the line as it built up. A full line was 1,600 hooks long and with a good fathom between each of the snoods represented almost two miles of line. A trough could take half of this comfortably, and the best of them, say the Spurling's, whose father was a carpenter and a boat–builder, could have floated the baby Moses himself down the Nile.

Billy and John started with about two hundred and fifty hooks, and by the time Mr Johnston made the trough for them, had increased it to some odd figure, three hundred and fifty three I think. When John went to England and Billy took me on as a substitute the line was already much longer than that. But some of the older, English twine was rotten, and Billy and John had lost a couple of sections, fastened in the bottom the previous year, so the first few days were spent bending on hooks and snooding up an extra couple of hundred fathoms of line. When we were ready we had eight hundred and eighty hooks. And I was only thirteen years of age.

Now there's a funny thing. All my life I have maintained and remembered it as thirteen years of age, but when I set to thinking about it recently, that was the summer Billy finished his first year at university. That would have made him eighteen, and me fourteen. Now I don't feel half as heroic. At fourteen I was well fit for anything that happened.

From the time I was five or six years of age and big enough to be taken out in the boat, I saw anything to do with the sea as an adventure. My favourite thing at that time was to be hunkered down on the bow-board with the stem at my back and my head tucked in under the breast-hook. As the bow rose and plunged into the waves, I could quite literally feel the slosh of the water on the other side of the planks. On the calm days, the sound was of a quiet rippling that sharpened into a little surge of noise with every pull of the oars and faded into a soft sibilance on the back-strokes. Fish were something else again, from the first gleaming quivering iridescent mackerel I ever caught – it jumped off the seat and smacked me in the puss – to the monster five and a half lbs. plaice that Billy and I hauled up one day on the long-line. The spots on it were redder than fresh rust, and every one of them as big as a Queen Victoria silver crown.

Billy was tough. Everything had to be just right even to the way the hooks were baited, with the needle-sharp point of the number nineteen haddock hooks skewered into the big juicy lug-worm just behind the head, then dipped and dipped repeatedly through the black or dark-red skin. My grandfather McKenzie was called the boss, as indeed was my other grandfather, the boss Hayden. The title seemed to have skipped a generation and landed on Billy. Even by the age of eleven, he too was the boss. That's just how he was with me. If I didn't hold the boat up just so, especially when we were hauling, he let me know. But he taught me, and I learnt. How to hold a mark – Harmon's red barn on the gap in the trees was our favourite for the biggest plaice – even when the boat slid down into the trough of the waves. How to row true by watching the wake astern when our head was for the shore. Where to find the best lug worms on Merrion strand. We travelled almost daily on the train with our spades and our bait cans to Blackrock, except for days when the tides didn't suit well. For these occasions we usually dug the baiting of the line twice on the previous day.

One thing I learned had nothing to do with instruction, and only incidentally to do with fishing, but it has stayed with me all my life. A year or two before I started fishing, Billy and John had bought an outboard motor, a one-and-a-half horsepower British Anzani. Whatever use it was when the two of them were fishing, it was as temperamental as hell in this particular year. And when Billy was swinging away on the lanyard, and swearing when it whipped him about the legs, I was rowing away. Ever since, I have distrusted technology and this has left me old-fashioned but, by God, I learned to rely on myself. I can still remember that it took 28 strokes to row from one telegraph pole to the next as we skirted the railway along the south beach on our way in from fishing.

I can't remember now how many weeks we fished, but it was the summer of Billy's first year at university. He was doing civil engineering and wanted above all else to get work somewhere in an engineering office and Kildare County Council offered him a summer job.

The day before he was to go away, the tide was right to go to fish about six o'clock in the morning. On the previous day we had dug the baiting of the line twice and then, having taken the morning shot on this last day, were determined to have one final extra shot at about half six in the evening. It would be more accurate to say Billy was determined because he had already suggested I keep on fishing with John Whiston, now that I knew the "marks". Half six in the evening was just about as late as we would want to go. What with it taking about three-quarters of an hour to get to the ground, another half an hour shooting, and an hour to fish, there wouldn't be much daylight left for hauling.

And we would be alone on the ground; the one other boat that was fishing lines that year would not be out. It was being fished by Larry Ryan – he was the king of longlinemen – together with Joe Sweeney and Ned Doyle.   They had a sixteen-hundred-hook line apiece and normally made only one shot a day. And they had already shot and hauled that morning.

I know it was a fine evening as we pulled away from the slip because I was wearing only a shirt and a pullover and a pair of short pants and, although I had a pair of sandals in the bow, I was in my bare feet. And for once the wee outboard motor fired up on the first pull. If it hadn't started I doubt if Billy would have gone, at least not to the Kilcoole grounds. We scarcely had the two halves of the line shot when the prospect for the evening changed in an ominous kind of way. The sky started to darken all over and the waves shortened in out of the Northeast. Without any more ado Billy decided to haul, even though the ebb hadn't fully gone. I did my best on the oars but, under the lowering sky, the run of the line was difficult to see, and even more difficult to follow, what with the contrary tide and the seas rising with the wind. We scarcely had three lengths in when the line broke. This time, there was no recrimination from Billy, just a terse under-breath kind of exclamation; more relief than annoyance.

"We'll leave the line", he said. "If we go to the other end, we might burst again and lose it. You can get John Whiston to haul it tomorrow, or whenever it clears." And he bent down immediately to prime the carburettor.

The Anzani started on the first pull and I shipped the oars.

"I think we'll head in for the shore" – still a good mile away – said Billy, "just in case." And I set about clearing what fish we had caught off the line and "gowing" up the hooks. And then I just sat there as the night darkened in on us, and paid little heed to Billy bailing. The "Kathleen" was nearly fifty years old and was rented in both the garboard and the bilge strakes, and I was accustomed to Billy's regular bailing. But this night it was more continuous; and it was with the spare bait can – a gallon tin.

We hit the shore somewhere about the second black hut. These were railwaymen's huts, the first at Ballygannon Point, and the second almost at the piles. There were two figures down on the beach ahead of us; we had seen them there from quite a long way off. The two were my father and Tommy Moran. As we came close to the shore, we could see that the bootlace weed – "fong" we called it – was showing on the low water despite the storm and was calming the breakers. Billy was wary of it, no matter what, and was afraid of going inside it in case it would foul our propeller. And that's how we went, labouring our way northwards; Billy bailing steadily; father and Tommy Moran gesticulating and shouting at us from the shore; and the waves continuing to crash in across the bow. Without any bidding from anybody, I put the spurs carefully into the "relicks" and slid out the pair of paddles. Slowly, we made our way northwards along the beach, past the "Money" river, past the outlet of the "Threetrout", past the culvert.

In the deeper water beyond the Swan's rock, we had a little consultation, Billy leaning forward to me and shouting above the wind, me leaning aft across the oars, straining to pick up whatever he was saying. The waves were steeper here than we had expected and I noticed he was bailing more than ever. Father and Tommy Moran, who had kept pace with us, trudging the two bicycles along the beach, were more urgent in their gesticulations. Here we could see them more clearly in the light of Wallace's coalyard and of the first light on the seafront.

"I'm afraid the boat will capsize on us if we attempt to beach her. And there's always the danger of getting fouled up in the hooks."

Billy looked at me:

"We'll have to go out to sea to clear the rocks at the back of St. David's. The cove won't be too bad but, with the weather out of the Northeast, we'll have to keep well out to clear the backwash off the pier. And if the outboard motor stops …"

I knew the question that didn't need to be asked. "If it stops, I'm ready. I can handle her." With no further consultation, that's what we did.

The little Anzani, whose unreliability so influenced me all my life, never faltered for a moment; not in the sharp overfalls at the back of St. David's; not in the last quarter mile until we turned, having waited a slow half minute or two to judge the wave right, some two or three hundred yards clear of the harbour; not even when we stuck the 'Kathleen's stem in the sand just short of the slip on the low tide. It was half past one in the morning, a full three hours, and maybe three and a half, maybe four miles since we left the Kilcoole grounds.

We didn't know it then, but that's the night we cast our bread upon the waters, and the Lord whistled up a storm and threw it, and us, right back onto the shore again.

My father is dead these thirteen year now. He died in the car on the way to Birmingham Airport, beside my youngest brother Declan, on the way home to the wedding of the first of his grandchildren to get married. Tommy Moran is still alive. I must go visit him. To thank him. He wouldn't have expected it, but it's time.

.

Chapter Eleven - War

Brian Stephens told us he had seen the soldiers marching across the sky at night, with blazing red eyes, carrying great rifles and bayonets in their hands. Brian's surname was really Stephenson, but we always used the handy version. We were just passing Dr Heaney's on our way home from school the day he told us. That was at the corner of the Church Lane, where it meets the road running across the top of Blacklion towards Killincarrig. On the opposite side of the main road at the T-junction was the old schoolhouse, and backing onto the school - yard was the clay-walled house where Dempsey Connolly lived. We never knew it was a clay walled house until Richie Doyle's house, one of the adjacent cottages, and part of Dempsey's grandmother's house washed down in a flood.

We were coming from school, Brian Stephens and I, and I'm not sure if Paddy Murphy wasn't among the others who were with us that day. I don't remember which school or class we were coming from; whether it was from first class, which was taught by Sister Mary Anthony in the convent; or from second or third class, both of which were taught by Brother McInerney in the supper room in St. Killian's hall. If you were to press me, I would probably say it was from Sister Mary Anthony's class, and I would probably be wrong. But one thing for sure, it was still wartime. When Brian and his pals had turned the Killincarrig direction towards lower Kendalstown and 'Crow Abbey' where they lived, and when we had turned towards my house – only a hundred yards the other way – and St Bridgid's Terrace beyond it, we talked about how big a liar Brian was, for such a small fellow. But the nights were darker, more fearful for us, afterwards. We knew there was a war over there.

Even today I don't know if Mrs Connolly was Dempsey Connolly's mother or grandmother. That she appeared to us an old lady has no particular significance; we were so young that all grown-ups were 'old'. What signifies for me though is that Connolly's house was one I was in and out of when I was small, and that what sticks in my mind is an image of a neat room with one small window deeply recessed into the wall, with most of the light coming from the open top part of the half-door. I could only bet that the colour of the door was dark-green, as was the colour of the door on some bit of a two-storey structure across what Donegal people call the 'street'. I have an impression of darkness, but I think this is just in my memory, and of Mrs Connolly being somehow a small dark old lady.

There were other such 'old' ladies that we knew when we were growing up, widows mostly, and it was perhaps the darkness of their clothes that has left this perception of darkness with me. The old cottages that some of them lived in may have been part of the reason – I don't suppose the windows in Mrs Connolly's were bigger than three foot high by two and a half foot wide, if that; nor were those in old Mrs Lynch's at no.1 or Kate Doyle's at No. 10 in the Bawn – but the power of the electric lights in use at that time was also part of the reason. Twenty-five watt bulbs were common; forty watt, the next up on the scale; sixty watt unthinkably powerful; and fifteen watts were available for those whose means didn't run even to the twenty-five.

It was sometime in the nineteen eighties that I first saw a print of John Keating's painting "Quench the lamps". I was visiting one of the older ESB offices on Merrion Square on fish farm business. The person I was meeting that day was a Mr. Barney Whelan, then chief biologist with 'Salmara', the ESB's fish farming subsidiary. When I remarked on how taken I was with the picture, he explained that it was a print of one of a series of paintings commissioned by the Free State government to mark the enterprise that was then called simply 'The Shannon Scheme'. The Ard-na-crusha project cost forty per cent of gross domestic product, an enormous sum. The picture in question is a dark, brooding, allegorical piece; appropriately powerful; not everyone's taste today, nor easily understood.. Neither will my memories of Mrs Connolly's or of Kate Doyle's cottages be easily understood. Mrs Connolly's was cleanly whitewashed without, with a neatly painted half-door and a thatched roof the edge of which, even as a child, I could reach, to search for birds nests in the holes that ran up into the straw. Kate Doyle's. I remember for the climbing roses that survived both the hens and the harsh sea air. Keating knew the darkness of the past but painted the promise of future light enigmatically. I saw the light, the colour, about me with the see-everything eyes of a child sent on errands – for some roses to fill a vase perhaps – yet have carried down the years with me a sense of a particular darkness, of an extra burden of poverty laid on people who had not much to start with, by a war that even as a child I was conscious of.

When I talked to John Connolly, Mrs Connolly's grandson and almost my own age, to check my facts in writing this chapter, he confirmed my own memories of the little complex of cottages, and much else besides. Most interesting of all was that he had a receipt issued to his grandmother dated 1922 for the amount of eight pounds for the purchase of the two storey structure, which was no more than one room up and one room down. This was where John's Uncle Willie lived. Willie Connolly was the hackney man that drove my father and Jimmy Lot to the mail-boat the night they went away to the war.

My child's consciousness was deepened for me in a particular way by my father going to the war. My Mother, left at home with three small boys and an infant daughter, still found it necessary to work, and consequently helped my Grandfather McKenzie in the shop; and because the shop was immediately adjacent to the convent school, I was enrolled there at the age of two and a half. I can remember eating 'Kimberley' biscuits and drinking a glass of milk for my lunch in my grandfather's parlour – a small room that was three steps down at the back of the shop and that was also darkly furnished – and then there were years and years, until almost nineteen forty eight, when 'Kimberley' were not on the market. I had to make do with fig-rolls.

But I learned to read early and, with what few comics and magazines that were on the market at that time available to me in the shop, was superficially ahead of my years.

The notable English magazines of the time were 'Illustrated' and 'Picture Post'. 'Illustrated' pioneered the publication of colour photographs. Years later, I chanced to be in the company of a mixum bunch of Irish people who had been invited on a familiarisation trip to the United States to Hyannis in Cape Cod. A fortuitously accidental meeting with a Dick Gallagher who was caretaker of the Kennedy properties in Hyannisport, led to the group being invited, not just into the compound, but into the family house itself, with the old lady upstairs in bed. When we were shown Rose Kennedy's collection of dolls I was able instantly to recognise two of the earliest as dolls of the young princesses Elizabeth and Margaret from the photographs I had seen in Illustrated of the blue school-uniformed princesses forty five years earlier. The moment was deliciously ironic: I was perhaps the only anti-Royalist in the group.

'Picture Post' was a different magazine entirely, and justifiably world-famous. When the Hulton magazine finally ceased publication, the 'Post' had amassed a library of some five million superb black and white photographs. As an archive of Britain's depressed thirties, and as a chronicle of World War II and its aftermath, it can scarcely be equalled. The collection survives today, bought initially I think by the Beatles' investment company 'Apple', which itself was bought by some other pop 'Superstar'. I am still occasionally reminded, by the publication of old photographs, of its pictures of London in flames during the blitz, of convoys of ships at sea, of streams of bombs dropping vertically onto landscapes and townscapes photographed from the very planes that dropped them, and of the mushroom bursts of their impact.

No pictures however equalled the horror of the images recorded at Belsen concentration camp, the first of the camps to be encountered by the Allied forces in the West. These were the first such photographs to be published. I cannot tell you how these affected me, but I cried for them a second time when death was dealt out again in the same way in the break-up of Yugoslavia; yet again when half-a-million were massacred in Rwanda and Burundi. Cried in horror and helplessness. Christ said "Weep not for me but for yourselves and for your children".

In the fiftieth anniversary year of the ending of World War two I set out for Poland to say a prayer of remembrance at Auschwitz concentration camp; to pray there for those for whom there no longer was anyone who could remember who even they were. In all those intervening years I had felt cut off from Europe; had seen the way in which we in Ireland distanced ourselves not just from the horror of war, but from any need to take a moral, informed position. Our neutrality then was in the light of our recent previous history understandable; conveniently strategic even. Our neutrality since has seemed spurious, a sham, a retreat from moral obligation. I had always wanted to travel, and in the later years of my career succeeded in doing so beyond anything I could ever have expected. I made it to USA, to Iceland, to Iran and to Chile; closer to home, to France, Denmark, Holland, Portugal, Spain; but for all of that I felt I only touched Europe on the periphery. That thing within still said I was isolated from the centre of Europe.

In 1990 I visited the Soviet Union and travelled by train from Moscow to Leningrad, then to Kandalaksha on the Western horn of the White Sea, and finally to Murmansk, the most northerly ice-free port in Europe. This was the destination of the grim twelve-knot convoys that kept Russia supplied with desperately needed war materials. While there, I was respected for proposing a toast to the Seamen who perished in those convoys – I had worked in Scotland on a fisheries research vessel and a fisheries cruiser that had both been built originally for escort duties on this run - and was invited to visit their graves.

But it was in Kandalaksha that I came closest to the Europe of that era. Visiting a metalworks factory that had then made bombs, grenades and other weapons, but that now made steel trawl-doors, aluminium net floats, diesel engine cylinder liners, our party was introduced by the Managing Director to his interpreter. His name was Alexander. She was cross and rebuked him using the familiar form of his name "But Sasha, I will not be adequate, I will not know the technical terms. Your wife speaks much better English than I. She has a university education". She was the English teacher in the local school, but had never met a native English-speaker. We were invited to visit the school after our business was done, and were entertained in the history room, the walls of which were covered with accounts of 'The Great Patriotic War, 1942-1945'. It felt like 1950.

In 1995 I wondered even myself if I was doing the right thing in going to Poland. I was very slow to actually make the move to go. In the end I went at a week's notice, towards the end of October, by coach from London to Krakow, having broken my journey in London to visit my Aunt Eileen who was then 92, and my daughter Eimear. It was a personal pilgrimage but, while I hadn't intended to fast, I found the need to cover a thousand miles from Calais to Krakow in 24 hours left no time for meal stops.

Jewish men, women and children who were shipped to Birkenau, without even the care you would give to animals, were sometimes eight or even ten days in transit, without food, without water, just without.

I walked past the infamous siding where they were literally stripped out of the wagons, to be forced physically to strip, and driven brutally into one of the two underground gas chambers. The immensity of the camp, more than four hundred acres – two thirds of a square mile – astounded me. It extended either side of the railway siding; and although the siding lay in full view of the camp, it was isolated from it on both sides by a double electrified fence which, even fifty years later, still stands with wire and insulators intact. The re-enforced concrete posts protrude to this day, deliberately left untouched, even from the International Memorial to the Jewish victims of the Holocaust.

The enormity of the crime – in scarcely a thousand days, more than one and a half million Jews were gassed and their bodies burnt; on one day alone as many as sixty thousand – could only be marked by touching not one stone, not one brick, not one strand of wire of such a terrible 'Páirc an Áir'. This was Birkenau, Auschwitz II.

The original Auschwitz, a captured Polish army barracks, seemed almost a practice camp, taking for its victims initially Poles, Gypsies and Jews alike, yet twenty thousand people were shot by firing squad – 'punishment' killings – at one four metre section of wall. I prayed there in the cell where Father Maximilian Kolbe, the Franciscan champion of the Immaculata, was starved, beaten, suffocated and ultimately murdered by lethal injection. He had in 1938 founded a house at Nagasaki, on the other side of a hill from the main centre of the city. It was his 'brothers' who tended the survivors of that new holocaust.

The Sunday after my visit to the camps I attended mass at the Mariacki Church in the centre of medieval Krakow. The abruptly interrupted trumpet tune that is repeated four times in succession every hour, from each of the four faces of the clock tower, is a reminder of how far the Tartars came in a previous age of War. When during the mass we were invited to share with one another a sign of peace, people merely turned to one another and bowed slightly. Was this fifty years, or five hundred years later?

Chapter Twelve – And No Further?

Parnell's hand, in the frozen space-time continuum of every Irish Christian Brothers boy, points forever to Mooney's pub in Upper Parnell St. I am talking of course of the hand of the statue at the Parnell Monument in Upper O'Connell St. Dublin. The universality of teaching of this 'fact' suggests almost that this was a basic tenet of our history as taught by the Brothers. Underneath the monument, the inscription on the plaque reads: "No man hath the right to set a boundary to the path of a nation. No man hath the right to say"Thus far shalt thou go, and no farther"! I have often wondered if Irish memory is a loop of tape only eight words long.

At a time when as a nation we had just written ourselves a 'national' constitution that held within it some good principles, but which we hedged about so with cavill and caveat that it was never possible to construct a code of positive law based on it, our 'national' parliament debated the exact number of ounces and fractions of ounces of sugar that might be allowed each citizen as his or her emergency wartime ration. The record is there. Go read it.

The fact that I was born in the year, 1937, in which our constitution was adopted gives me no special insight to and no greater understanding of that particular document. It establishes only that I was a child of those times, and have grown into these. Just over fifty years on from the debate on the wartime sugar ration, a more contentious matter was occupying our elected representatives. The beef industry, which had been the mainstay of our agriculture for so long, had its problems, scandals even, and Government and Ministers were scurrying for cover. At a particularly awkward time, an extraneous matter got thrust into the Nation's centre of attention. A forty-year plus married man had been carrying on with a fourteen-year-old girl, the daughter of friends. A sad, anger-making thing. Not, unfortunately, all that uncommon in our society now or in the past; nor indeed in other societies. All of a sudden a conflation of different interests coalesced about this singular item of news reported by a media whose journalists were pledged to support the ready availability of abortion. A year or so on and the Irish public were again presented with a plethora of referenda, the beef scandal already pushed to the back of memory.

A proposal to restrict the availability of abortion was defeated. An earlier referendum to protect the life of the unborn child had been written into the constitution, but the news reportage of the 'X'case – the fourteen year old and the forty year plus married man – had so influenced the women of Ireland that one could almost feel them abandon the starboard rail and move to port. A right to information amendment was passed; that is, a right to information about abortion. So also was a right to travel amendment; a right to travel to procure an abortion. I personally thought that for any Irish government to even suggest that they had the right to stop Irish people travelling, in a country in which one in every two Irish people born in this century had to emigrate, was obscene.

Six years earlier a friend, a businessman, from Sweden was visiting Donegal. He was a founding director of the company I then worked for, and of which I later became Managing Director. His own, almost one hundred year old family business in Sweden had experienced difficulties, and he had committed himself to one years extremely stressful work to overcome them. At the year-end accounting he left the tally to his auditors and retreated to Donegal to get away from the tension of it all. For him, sharing a moment and a gin and tonic in the Nesbitt Arms in Ardara was a medicine of wonders. One afternoon, after touring West Donegal from Gweedore to Killybegs in a borrowed car, he asked me about the houses and bungalows he had seen right through the countryside – they had impressed him so much – and what work the people had that could afford such fine houses. How much more would he now be impressed, twelve years later? Mangan's vision of Connaught in the thirteenth century, a poem commended to me years ago by a

Dublin lad named Leo whom I met when both of us were trying to sell vacuum cleaners, would scarcely compare.

Had my Swedish friend toured a different county twelve years back the other direction in time he might have seen a different picture of Ireland. I had at that time come to live in Falcarragh in north-west Donegal and had settled in it as if it were home. I worked twelve miles away on the Industrial Estate in Gweedore.

In 1974 I was made redundant but having lived through the trauma of my parents enforced emigration was determined not to move at that time. I was very conscious of doing this to protect my family. Sometime the following year I got a temporary job as an area supervisor on the first of what came to be known as the 'Labour Force Surveys'. I answered to a regional supervisor who happened to be one of those rare individuals who could interface between bureaucracy and ordinary people without losing his own integrity. The concern was to do a thorough job and achieve as high a level of accuracy and completion as possible. But inevitably some people declined to be interviewed, and others could not be located. Because it bore on the method of payment to the interviewers in the particular areas, we supervisors usually tried to establish why a house, which was perfectly habitable, might have no one living in it. The answers were fascinating. In one of my areas, nineteen percent of the houses were owned by people from Derry. In another, the area with the greatest 'absentee' ownership, twenty four percent in total, the almost entirely new houses were owned by people from Belfast. Except that was, for a four percent of local ownership where the families had simply moved away.

In another part of the country an interviewer found house after house, traditional homes, where the door had merely been pulled out, and the breakfast plates with the dried-up remains of the last meal had been simply left on the table. It was families such as these that I had seen on each of the twelve crossings of the Irish Sea that I made between nineteen fifty-five and nineteen sixty. I crossed twice on the Dublin-Glasgow run, and once Larne-Stranraer, but I think those crossings happened later in the sixties. The earlier crossings were almost all on the Dunlaoghaire-Holyhead run; on the mail-boat. Each time I would already have boarded by the time the boat train pulled out the Carlyle pier and discharged the country passengers. The sight of families finding their way about the unfamiliar craft, and the way they settled down with cups of British Railways tea, each group in its own kind-of private party, was something that became familiar, something not easily forgotten. Tony Callaghan from Killybegs, a friend I made later in life, said to me on one occasion on which I was discussing some of the chapters of this book that he often felt I had unresolved, unfinished, business with the Irish State. My reply was immediate: "Yes. Absolutely". I went on to say that I would like to drive all politicians before me with a rolled-up Sunday Newspaper. I don't think I said more, other than to try and explain how I felt those who should have been our leaders lost hope on us, and in us, in the nineteen fifties. I suppose I find it hard not to believe they could do so again.

One lingering image from the 'Manpower' survey is of a fine, red-granite wall-stead somewhere on a bog road above Kincasslagh, perfect in every way except that there was no roof on it. The roof pegs – shafts of stone set into the wall at regular intervals along the length of the house just below the roofline, on to which tyings would be made to secure the thatch – were as clean-cut as when the house had been built. Maybe I too fear being a shell of eloquence.

Chapter Thirteen – Sugar and Spice

I don't believe any food shop smelled cleaner than a Hafners pork-butchers shop. There were five of them in the city of Dublin, but the one I mostly went into was at the bottom end of Henry Street. In a sense one could almost say the building had no smell, so clean were the tiled walls and the marble-slabbed counters, but the first thing one noticed on coming into the shop was the faint tang of the freshly scattered and newly milled sawdust. The total image was of cleanliness. Well-washed faces on the women serving behind the counter, and no make-up. Hands to match, and spotlessly white shop-coats and aprons. No plastic gloves I can assure you; such dreadful things. Joints of pork, palest pink with a decent rim of white fat; the leg, shoulder and collar joints wrapped in a scalded scrubbed and shaven ivory-coloured skin that would crisp up in roasting to the most delicious cracknel. I could distinguish between the smell of the newly prepared black and white puddings and that of the glistening pink sausages that were delivered daily in scoured aluminium tubs. I swear I could even smell the aluminium. What a mistake the William's supermarket chain made when they bought the shops apparently thinking to capitalise only on the sausages and the name. Mind you the name counted for a good deal. A friend I made, Ronnie Brenner, whom I first met and worked with when we were both draughtsmen in the Irish Glass Bottle Co., and whose parents had a pork-butchers shop in Pearse St., told me much about the making of sausages and puddings. He told me also of a government regulation that had been made - during the 'Emergency' I think – stipulating the minimum percentage of meat allowable in a sausage. Hafners were able to show from their records that they had consistently made their sausages with a lower percentage, and so were allowed derogate from this requirement, and they still sold at a premium price. As the Americans might say; neat.

I was well practised at shopping in Hafners. Very occasionally I shopped in the South Great Georges St. shop, but it was rather small and a string of a queue tended to tail out through the door. The shop in Talbot St. commonly had a bit of a queue also, but my favourite was the shop at the bottom of Henry Street, almost directly across the road from one of the Dublin Bacon Company shops. The Henry street Hafners was well staffed and had plenty of room for customers who simply pressed in three deep all along the counter. I was a slim young fellow and could edge my way easily into the cracks and crevices of this human wall. On one occasion when I managed to slip into a gap between two women who were already at the counter, and in front of a rather fat lady, I was given a good reminder to take my manners with me the next time when I got a quare good thump from her shopping basket in the small of the back. By 1953/54 when my Mother had already taken over the shop from my grandfather, and when I was in an 'idle' year, between finishing secondary school and attempting University, I was regularly buying thirty five pounds weight of Hafner's sausages every Friday for our shop, and a similar weight of narrow back rashers from Sheil's of Moore Street. My contact in Sheil's was a man called Jimmy Seery whom my mother first met when he worked in Talbot Street in the 'Big Bear' which was the first shop in Ireland to style itself a supermarket. But although it was fitted out with chrome railings, and a 'stile' type access gate, the staff just served you the same as in any other shop.

I can only suppose it was because the 'Big Bear' was so near Tara Street or Amien's Street stations that my Mother shopped there in the first place; it wasn't so far for carrying heavy parcels. It may also have had to do with the relative frequency, or comfort, of the train vis a vis the bus during the war. Later on she found the bus more convenient, especially as it stopped at the door of the shop for both inward and outward journeys. By the time I did the heavy hauling for her, the bus was by far the best option because of Byrne's newspaper and confectionery shop at the starting point of the no.84 bus in College Street. For a small charge the shop would mind parcels for people intending to travel later. My own errands sometimes involved three or four treks with 'messages'; items as diverse as a couple of twenty-eight lb. cartons of butter and maybe a box of Cleeve's toffee from O&R Fry in Hawkins Street; or plug tobacco from the marvellously scented factory of Taylor Brothers in Townsend Street. There was another tobacco factory at Tailors Hall in Francis Street in the Liberties but I cannot now remember the name of it. I knew where to shop for buttons and ribbons – in a little shop up the quays – and my way in and out of various wholesale departments from Eason's on Middle Abbey Street to Willwoods & Clarnico Murray at the top of Upper Parnell Street; even as far as Rowntree – Macintosh in Kilmainham. The 'Big Bear' sticks in my mind most particularly though for my first sight of Dublin Street urchins sucking lemons, the time they came in first after the war. The kids were hanging about some street stalls that were selling oranges and lemons, and my throat still purses dry at the thought of the sucked lemons.

The first day the oranges came into my grandfather's shop at the end of the war, he cleared eleven cases by five o'clock in the afternoon, and he had sold all sixteen cases, all that he was allowed, by evening. He did something similar the day the dried fruit came in, clearing fifteen or sixteen boxes of raisins, currants and sultanas in the one afternoon. Rice puddings became something different, almost exotic, for us. Baked in the oven; an egg lightly beaten in through the milk, and two handfuls of black raisins stirred into the rice; nutmeg, real whole nutmeg, grated over the top of the mixture. Scraping the last rim of skin off the empty dish was the real bonus, and we clamoured for it. As children of the age that we were at, we should scarcely have known that we were deprived of anything, but somehow or other we did. And did without feeling grieved over it, so that when these marvels – oranges, lemons, sultanas and raisins; extra supplies of jam even – happened to us, it was wildly exciting. Jam was nine-pence – old pence, mind you – a one pound pot, and either one and thruppence or one shilling and sixpence for a two pound pot. The two-pound pot was better, because it was easier to scrape the last skim of jam off the inside of the jam-jar when the pot was almost empty. We had other ways of measuring the excitement of those days also. From the harbour we tallied the ships riding at anchor in Dublin Bay waiting to get into the port. On one day alone we counted forty-eight.

Do you know the funny thing though about those first oranges? They were Spanish oranges, and they were as bitter as hell. It didn't stop our Mother squeezing them for juice to top-up the spoon of castor-oil that in those days was deemed a regular necessity to keep us regular. To this day I find it hard to look a glass of freshly squeezed orange juice in the face.

How quickly we became accustomed to the exotic newness of these gorgeous things; bananas; other, sweeter varieties of oranges; thick-skinned Jaffa's from Palestine; half-red 'blood oranges' from Spain; whole nutmegs and a range of spices; tangerines and boxes of dates at Christmas; white bread. The wartime 'black' flour was a dismal grey sort of a mixture, well adulterated with finely ground bran. The day the new 'white' loaves were permitted, I can remember being sent to my uncle Johnny McKenzie's shop in Blacklion for a couple of loaves of bread. I can't now remember whether they were pan-loaves, batch loaves, or turnovers, but I had two great holes picked in the loaves by the time I got over the road home. My Grandfather McKenzie was reared in an even more frugal time, and with Scots blood on both sides – Gilbert and Mckenzie – saved the beautifully scented tissues that the oranges were wrapped in, for use as disposable handkerchiefs. That was long before they boxed and sold them.

I had helped, as had Billy and John, in the shop whenever our Mother asked us to; mostly on my part weighing up tea, sugar and flour. I can still remember how much I liked the crinkly, preformed double-skinned tea bags, and often wish I could still buy 'loose' tea just as easily. Earlier still, at home in Blacklion, we were shown how to cut out the necessary coupons from the ration – books, and we passed many an evening snipping away with the scissors after our lessons were done. In the shop, the tea, sugar and flour were kept right at the back at one side of the steps leading down to the parlour. The sugar came in a sixteen stone sack, and to this day I don't know where my five foot seven inch grandfather got the strength to manoeuvre it. The flour was in a more standard one-cwt bag, a fine cotton bag, but was almost as bulky as the sack of sugar. The standard container for the tea was a lead-foil lined plywood tea chest, that when I was only six or seven reached just above my belly button. I never smoked pot, or did drugs in my life, but I can tell you nobody ever got a 'kick' like I did when I was balancing on my belly on the rim of the tea-chest, trying to scoop up the last few tea-leaves from the bottom of the chest, and inhaling the dust of a fine black Indian tea. Hallelujah, Sahib!

The butter and the cheese, such as it was - no more than a round of hard cheddar, or a seven lb. box of foil-wrapped 'plastic' cheese – were in the same corner of the shop but on the counter to the front, adjacent to the scales. The butter in a huge cake was tumbled from a twenty eight-pound butter-box into a porcelain tray that sat just in front of the cheddar cheese, with two wooden butter paddles in a jug of water beside it. Before the war, my father must have made three little seats from butter-boxes for Billy, John and myself, because I have images in my mind of them yet, although my images are of John, myself and Kathleen playing with them in the house in Blacklion. On the other side of the steps to the parlour at the back of the shop was kept a sack of porridge oats, and usually a half-bag of pinhead oatmeal for customers who kept hens. All this was very vulnerable to foraging mice, you might think, but my grandfather enforced a regime of zero-tolerance; long before the New Yorkers thought they had invented it. My grandfather's secret weapon was unpatented, and probably unpatentable. Whenever he detected even the slightest sign of a mouse, he would leave a biscuit tin filled with scrunched-up crinkly paper – greaseproof paper, maybe from empty biscuit tins, was best – lying on its side, with a trickle of porridge oats or biscuit crumbs leading into the tin, somewhere near the sacks of sugar and flour. When he heard a rustle of paper, he simply clamped the lid on the tin, and took it outside to dispose of the mouse. I've done it myself, and it works.

There were, occasionally, mice who made it to the high shelves where the packets of cocoa and Farola and dried peas were stacked. For these, the mousetrap with the springloaded wire nooses, that had to be tied down by a couple of strands of sewing cotton, was the answer. The wire nooses could move up and down in individual slots in a solid block of wood into which a number of holes had been drilled. Baited with a few shavings from a bar of chocolate, they never failed. Should you ever be plagued with mice, forget the cheese or the bit of fried bacon, bait up with chocolate. The mice, poor creatures, are no better than ourselves; suckers with a sweet tooth; lining up with tightly clutched pennies for our 'Glory Balls', or our 'Nancy Balls' – aniseed, really – just as we did all those years ago. Glory Balls, which were coated with a deep red wine colour that could be licked to moisten it and then be smeared all over our lips, were solid little globules of rock-hard sugar that knocked chips off our teeth as we crunched them. Crunch them we did, and our 'Conversation lozenges'; and we chewed our five-a-penny toffees and our liquorice pipes.

These were available to us for the price of a penny; a ha'penny even, because my grandfather would give three toffees for a ha'penny.

Round about nineteen forty six or forty seven I made a friend of a young English lad named David Robinson, both of whose parents came from the five towns area of Staffordshire. Whatever year it was, by nineteen forty-eight the (Christian) Brothers were teaching us in our geography lessons of this special area in the middle of England known as the 'Potteries', or the 'Five Towns'. 'It was in the heart of the Black Country '. That self-same year an aunt and uncle of David's came on holiday to Ireland, and it was planned that David travel back with them to visit his grandparents; both sets of grandparents. Quite unexpectedly, but to my surprise and delight, I was invited to go with him. Our parents sorted out the business of getting travel permits, and we found it no time at all until we were on our way with David's aunt and uncle on the Dunlaoghaire – Holyhead mail boat; on the evening sailing. We were well accustomed to watching it from Greystones, all of twelve miles away from Dunlaoghaire, as it steamed out across Dublin Bay to the Kish light-ship, then head out to sea and go hull-down over the horizon; morning and evening. Now we were on it. Neither David nor his aunt or uncle knew that my mother had loaded me with a twelve pound rack of chops, practically a full side, of prime Wicklow mutton; and not satisfied with that, had topped it off with a fourteen-pound ham, which I carried in a shopping bag. And while David's uncle explained to the Welsh customs officer at Holyhead at about half-past midnight that we were just two young boys coming on holiday, I held out my bag and my case to have them chalked, contents undisclosed and undeclared, and carried on through the customs hall to the railway platform outside as if my two parcels were no more than two hanks of fish. It was years later that I watched Sam McAughtry, the Belfast author and TV personality, interview a former Northern Ireland customs officer who admitted to taking a contraband half a pound of cooked ham off some unfortunate cross border traveller and throwing it to the dog. No dog got mine I can assure you.

It was the following afternoon before we finally reached the home of David's Grandmother and Grandfather Robinson on the Milehouse Lane – I'd swear the house number was 172 –just outside Newcastle-under-Lyme. We had come via Crewe, then changed either at Stafford or Nuneaton onto a train for Stroke-on-Trent, then back on a commuter train to Etruria where the aunt and uncle lived. We travelled the final few miles from Etruria to Newcastle with David's uncle on a double-decker bus that was neatly appointed with slatted wooden seats. David's uncle was still with us when I unpacked my mother's gifts of mutton and ham. They were all stunned to silence.

David's grandparents told me later their weekly ration of bacon at that time was an ounce and a quarter per person. Few geographical names can so conjure up an exotic image as the 'Spice Islands'. Christian crusaders fought Islam more for the spice trade than for access to the Holy Land, and Christopher Columbus discovered an entire New World while trying to find a shorter route to them. The Robinsons in 1948 could easily have supposed that Ireland had momentarily become one of them.

You might well ask how the Robinsons connected to any of these things I have just been writing about. I believe the fourteen pound ham was bought by my mother from Jimmy Seery when he worked in the 'Big Bear' supermarket. As for the Robinsons themselves, they lived just across the road from a munition factory in which, so far as I'm aware, both of them worked during World War Two. Even yet, we still owe them.

Chapter Fourteen – White Bread and Blackberry Jam

There is no one left who can now tell us what it was like for our mother when she was growing up. By 1923, before she was yet even thirteen years old, her mother, Catherine McKenzie – her maiden name was Kinsella – had been buried in a plot in the old graveyard in Kilcoole. My grandmother's brother Michael Kinsella who was killed in World War One is buried either in the same grave or in the plot alongside. As a young girl, my mother must have come enormously under the influence of her aunts Lizzie, Mary Ann, and Winnie – who were all Kinsellas – and aunts Margaret and Sarah, who were married to Willie Kinsella and John Thomas Kinsella respectively.

For me, the influence of the aunts was most evident in my mother's skill as a baker. Both Aunt Lizzie and Aunt Mag – short for Margaret – were superb; one might almost say precision bakers. My mother was a bit more variable, but at her best she beat my two grandaunts into a cocked hat, to use a phrase from their time. My mother baked more often, in greater quantities, and attempted a wider variety of confections than either of my grand-aunts, so far as I was aware, but I'm certain she learned all from them in the first place. Who knows what she had also learned from her mother Catherine before her mothers illness.

Saturday afternoon was her time for baking when we were young. In wartime it was generally just bread and scones that she baked. But when she had sugar, butter, eggs and cooking apples available, we got the extra treats of queen cakes, Victoria sandwiches and apple tarts. On these occasions we – John, Kathleen and myself – would be set first to the task of sieving the 'black' wartime flour. This was an illegal activity. It had specifically been proscribed for the duration of the emergency, and young as we were, we knew this. It was the only activity ever in which our mother encouraged us to break the law. But let me tell you, the wartime 'black' flour needed sieving. It wasn't as if it was made by only partly removing the bran. It was more as if the bran was separated out as normal in milling, then very finely ground and blended back into the flour again. Bread made with it ended up a dirty, unappetising grey in colour; even bought bread.

In either 1944 or 1945, I cannot now tell you which, we must have had a really good summer that stretched out through August into September. Mother had a late letting for Novara, the house in Blacklion, and we were still in Mrs Archer's cottage in the Bawn. I was in either second or third class, both of which were taught by Brother McInerney in the supper-room of St Killian's, the parochial hall. Since the Brothers came, there just wasn't room enough in the old school in Blacklion. Living so close to school – the hall was only two hundred yards over the road from the Bawn – I would normally have run home at playtime, which was what we called the lunch-break, for my dinner. But I guess my mother wasn't making a dinner in the middle of the day due to the warm weather, and she made jam sandwiches instead. Now I guess my mother was absolutely fed-up with the dreary war-time bread and flour, and I suppose also, with the long-some separation from Father. On the previous Saturday she baked, in her two biggest cake tins, two beautiful golden brown loaves of white yeast bread. Kathleen and I, and John, I suppose, sieved the flour for her. In a two-room cottage. With a tiny range – the two cake tins were all the oven could hold. With no running water. And on the previous Saturday but one, she had taken us all blackberry picking up Pat Fox's fields at Coolegad, and had made blackberry jam. The sandwiches I had that next Monday were magic. I was eventually persuaded to swap one, only one mind you, with a pal. It could have been Paddy Redmond or Paddy Murphy, but isn't it funny it's really Peter Mitchell's name that comes into my mind when I think of it. Whoever it was, the sandwich he swapped was a lovely home-made brown bread sandwich. But the magic and the memory are of the white bread and the blackberry jam.

As I said at the start, we don't know what it was like for my mother when she was young, nor indeed what she was like. There are few photographs of her as a young woman, and the dual break in which Billy, John, Kathleen and I launched ourselves off into the world, as Mother and Father, Aunt Eileen, and the younger family had to move to England, created a gap which we were only starting to bridge again adequately in the few years before they died. We don't even know how exactly it was that she and Father connected in the first place. It was hardly at a dance hall. What was to become St. Killians Hall after an original hall was burnt down and rebuilt was then a 'Protestant' hall. It might have been at a farmhouse dance. My uncle Bernie always claimed the 1927 Dance Hall act, which required places of public entertainment to be licensed, brought about the end of rural social life. But my guess is that Mother and Father probably connected as young teenagers at Irish classes that were given by Mrs DeValera. The DeValeras lived in Greystones at the time and there was local popular support, especially for Mrs DeValera who was remembered always as being a 'lady'. The classes were seen as a way of financially supporting her while Dev was away or in prison, and both Mother and Father attended them.

Our mother had other suitors. One we know of was the son of a Dublin tailor who not only outfitted my grandfather, but also came with his family on holidays to Greystones. There was quite an understanding between our mother and one of his son's, apparently, but each made other marriages. Another different son followed the father in the business, both named Barney Lynch, and a third Barney followed on from them. I came to know Barneys two and three when they visited Greystones at the end of the 'forties, and rowed them out many a time for fishing and pleasure in our boat, the Kathleen. Our first tailored suits were all made in their draper's shop in Camden Street, as indeed was my own wedding suit. I have no doubt but that there is a fourth Barney Lynch carrying on the tradition, but it wasn't to become our tradition.

My mother chose Father. Aunt Lizzie, her godmother and mine, told me of Father's return from Australia. Two or three girls had notions of him. I think they all must have written to him, and he to them. But my mother was the only one who went to meet him off the mailboat at Dunlaoghaire when he returned home. She got him. But there was a day when she nearly lost him. It was Father's Godmother, Fan Donohoe who told me how close a call it was. Mother and Father had gone for a cycle one afternoon when they were courting and were returning to the village of Delgany either from Kilcoole or Kilquade direction. As Father sped down the steep brae at Stylebawn Glebe he looked back over his shoulder to tease Mother with "What's keeping you, McKenzie?" just as a donkey walked out the gate of a field in front of him. I don't know how far he flew but he was said to be unconscious for fourteen hours. I really know little more than that about my mother and fathers courtship, but they were two stories that influenced my very particular choice of words at Father's funeral when I said of my mother "The love for her life-long companion remains". That love, and that companionship, for each other and for their family, was tested as in a fire in 1957 when Mother was faced with the forced sale of her business. Father's disappointment at not being paid for four weeks hospitalisation, necessitated by an operation to remove a cyst on his back, didn't help. Father went ahead of her to England, financed by a loan from Aunt Lizzie, got a job in Watford, and found accommodation in an old artist's studio at Bushey in Hertfordshire. The studio was simply a tin barn with one great north light window, and a lean-to shed of a room at the gable that served as a bedroom. The main structure butted onto the back of a bungalow in which the landlady, a Mrs Potter who was a rather elderly widow, lived. A combination scullery cum cooking area under corrugated plastic at the side of the bungalow doubled also as the front entrance to the 'Studio Flat'. A side door off the studio gave access to the rear door of the bungalow, and also to the original outside toilet which now served the flat. The use of the bathroom in the bungalow was

89

allowed once a week. This was where they lived for six months after Mother followed Father to England. This was where Aunt Eileen, and young Eileen who was then only eleven, and my nine year old brother Barney who was born with Down's Syndrome, and my youngest brother, Declan, who was only three, came to live when I took them over six months later; and lived there for a further five and a half years. This is where I retreated and rolled mattress and blankets down on the floor as I tried again and yet again to get started in life on my own, and got knocked back each time. This was just one more burden in the life of this handsome woman who was my mother; who had been brought up to carry so much responsibility.

People who met my mother in middle life might not have seen how fine she looked when she was younger. The few photographs that we have from that earlier time convey an impression of character one would normally associate only with a portrait in oils. Later on the burdens of care and hard work set deep lines into her broad Kinsella face. In height she favoured my grandfather - its funny, in my life I met two other John McKenzies, and each had the same lack of height and slightness of build – but in her features, and in the strength of her bones, she was a Kinsella. Guessing games as to who favours whom in looks and character are a common preoccupation in most families, and equally inconclusive in all, but my mother lives in my youngest sister, Eileen. I am only just beginning to learn how close they became through odd shared moments, time-outs you might say, as my sister grew up in England.

My most intimate memory of my mother is of watching her brush her hair when I was very young. Her hair was dark in colour then and, brushed out, tumbled down her back to waist level. This she divided daily, plaited it into a long great pigtail, and wound it tightly into a bun which was pinned at the back, drawing the rest of her hair tight about her head. It made her look stern. There is a lovely photograph of her as a child with my grandfather and grandmother, which seems to have been taken in the parlour behind the shop. It is a photograph that pictures the promise of life to come, of the pleasures that may follow. I must look at it again; to know that there was a time in the innocence of her childhood when there could be no premonition of pain. I do know how she enjoyed herself; in her family, and in her family's families. When she died I can remember thinking how blessed she was; she saw all her children live and all her grandchildren. Few women in her time could say as much. She enjoyed a show – live on stage rather than a film. She once told me that the first film she ever saw, with Father, was Bela Lugosi's portrayal of 'Dracula' and she never really liked films afterwards.

As children, Billy, John, Kathleen and I were taken to pantomimes in Dublin, and whatever shows and concerts that were put on locally. I particularly remember a year when the Theatre Royal presented their panto in three shows daily, each show following continuously on the other in the manner of the normal cinema programme. I cannot remember what panto it was but Noel Purcell was the dame, as usual, and was partnered by Jack Cruise. On this occasion, however, they were joined by Cecil Sheridan who usually appeared in pantomime in the 'Olympia'. The 'Royal' was a huge theatre, seating just short of four thousand people, but we were late finishing our shopping and although we joined the queue for the second performance, all seats had sold out before we got to the box-office. I'm sure there were four of us, so it must have been Mother and I, Kathleen and a very young Eileen; and rather than disappoint us, Mother decided we would have our tea and come back for the last performance.

We didn't go very far for our tea. There was then a little café just across the street from the 'Regal Rooms' cinema, which adjoined the Theatre Royal. We enjoyed the experience of "eating out" in a café – I'm sure all we had was something like fried egg and chips – and made certain we got back in time to head-up the queue for the last performance. The ticket office opened early as patrons who had come in towards the end of the first performance left the theatre before the end of the second show. We came in just as the second last scene was beginning. Noel Purcell, the dame, was engaged with his henchmen, Jack Cruise and Cecil Sheridan, in the comic business of making a cake, with much shaking of flour and splashing of porter. Now the porter looked real, and it looked also as if as much was going inside the actors as went in the mixing bowl. When the final performance started Mother decided we would sit right through to the end again; the theatre would be warmer and more comfortable than waiting in the cold for a bus. By the time we got to the cake-mixing scene for the second time, the three comedians could hardly stand, forgot their lines, and had to make it all up as they went along. I don't think I ever laughed as much in a theatre. Our eyes were still running with tears of mirth as we walked across the road home at midnight from the last bus.

Ten years on from Mother's death I regret not availing of the opportunity to take her up to London to a show. The West End was just as near to Bushey as Dublin was to Greystones.

After six years in the studio flat, Mother was allocated a Council house, which Billy later bought out for her. Before that, round about 1960, a block of beautiful maisonettes was built almost across the road from the flat. They sold for three thousand eight hundred and fifty pounds. A lot at the time, perhaps, but it was certainly within the reach of Mother and Father's combined incomes. Not until I made a friend years later of a banker who was to become Allied Irish Banks number one man in Scotland did I appreciate the need of Irish people who had to emigrate for institutions they could identify with. When Bank of Ireland opened the first overseas branch of any Irish bank, in Kilburn, they took two million in deposits on the first day. But such support was late for my parents.

Mother was happy though in her Bushey home, and we all came and stayed with her from time to time, and brought our children, whom Auntie Eileen delighted to take away up Bushey Park to the paddling pool. When they grew bigger they managed the swimming pool on their own. Mother continued to work too hard in Mac Fisheries fruit and vegetable shops where she became first a Fruit Manageress, then a roving Area Manager. The Mac Fish system of management compared with our 'Points system'. I can remember my mother telling me in the early 1960's how she had done three hundred and sixty seven pounds for the week, and how, when she was congratulated by her supervising manager, the next question was "Do you think you can do three ninety next week, Annie?"

She suffered intermittently from ill health, most significantly from a medically unexplained propensity to blackouts. Overwork had to be a factor. Once, when I was living and working in Winsford in Cheshire, married with three small children, I got a letter one Tuesday telling how she had taken a haemorrhage at the weekend and had been ordered to bed by the doctor. The following morning, Wednesday, I was most unusually seriously late for work. As I crossed the main Liverpool- London railway, indicating left to turn at the next cross roads into the industrial estate where I worked, I started to think, "My mother is at work when she should be home in her bed". I knew I had a five pound note in my pocket, and that the day-return fare to London Euston, or to Watford Junction, was four pounds thirteen shillings and some odd pence. I looked at my watch. Thirty minutes to the time of the last morning express leaving Crewe; and I could make Crewe junction in twenty minutes. I didn't hesitate. I indicated and wheeled right, and gunned the Anglia.

When I came out of the railway station at Watford junction, there were no buses standing at the bus terminus. I was familiar with all of this; I had worked there as a railway porter in 1958. I decided to walk up Clarendon Road to Watford High Street to look at the shops, and as I got closer felt more and more that I would meet my mother. Sure enough, almost at the junction with Market Street my mother came along. "I was expecting to see you," she said.

Just over a year before Father died, he took a turn one night. Afterwards it seemed to me that he was perhaps sleeping on his back, and started to choke from the bronchitis he had. He was smoker of Woodbines since he was thirteen years old. He went into a kind of a rigor or spasm, fell out of the bed, hit his head on the chest of drawers, and knocked himself out. The fall broke the blockage in his breathing otherwise I'm sure he would have gone. Mother was very frightened. I hadn't visited them for quite some time, and felt bad for it. A question of opportunity and money. I was living on the edge of the ocean in West Donegal, in debt to the bank, under the pressure of educating a family; I took a week's holiday and travelled to Bushey just to be there for Mother.

She was coping as she had always coped; of necessity. Father was recovering and had signed himself out of hospital because they wouldn't let him smoke, but he was weak. She told me how Father's main concern as he recovered consciousness had been his modesty. He had always slept just in his shirt, and wouldn't let the ambulance man in until he got his underpants on. Mother said he was always a very modest man. The house as always was chock full of grub, and Mother insisted on either herself or Auntie Eileen cooking as normal. At bedtime, her bedtime, I was instructed to pour myself a whisky or cut a slice of fruitcake; both were in the sideboard in the front room. Her talent was for big fruitcakes, rising to six or seven inches, or even more. This was one such cake, but for lightness of crumb combined with moist rich fruit I simply have never eaten better. I think her baking and her cooking became a substitute for conversations that she could never have.

Before I left, I resisted the temptation on Sunday afternoon to go to Borehamwood to visit a former general manager of a company I worked for in Northwest Donegal, and who had become a good friend. "I came for my mother," I said to myself. She insisted on washing the dishes after lunch, and I sat to read the newspapers. The television was on at the same time. After a while she came into the living room and started to read a newspaper. Suddenly I was conscious of a deep silence. Even the television seemed hushed. I looked at my mother. She was as grey as a warship. One of her turns. The first time I had ever seen it happen. It was frightening.

The year she died I had been told by a business colleague of his plans to sail a yacht down to Portugal, and I asked if I could come along. I had not been at sea for years, had never sailed, and when I saw the light Mediterranean-built motor-sailer when I joined it in Connemara, was extremely jittery. A poteen session the night before we sailed, followed by a late poteen-and-fried-homecut-fat-rashers breakfast before we sailed didn't help much. Blows of adverse wind put us first into Kilronan, then into Castletownberehaven. I phoned home as Ann, my wife had suggested I do. Mother had suffered a stroke, in the tiny back garden among her flowers. It took me two days to get to London. Gales had closed Cork Airport. When I got to the hospital, Eileen and Declan were there ahead me, as was my nephew David. David was holding my Mother's hand, and I kind-of resented that. He was undergoing a major change in his life at the time and had come to Mother as so many of us had before him, but she no longer felt able for that. She had phoned me two weeks earlier to say so. But I knew he was only trying to comfort her. After a while, reassured by the nursing staff that she would be all right, that they did not think her condition would deteriorate, we slipped away back up to the house. Before we could get back to her, she too had slipped away.

As we carried her coffin into the cemetery to be buried with Father in Redford, my eye caught a name on a gravestone, Dick Rickman. Dick Rickman and his mother had been laid out on the fine linen sheets and with the blessed candles that Mother kept in the bottom drawer of her dressing table in the house in Blacklion. Dick used to do the garden for her; one day a week; she paid him a pound a day, a good day's wage in those days. I thought to myself "You have friends here before you".

Chapter Fifteen – "We're Your Friends"

If there had been a security camera, as has unfortunately become so necessary in many places today, at the road end of St. Bridgid's Terrace in Blacklion aroundabout 1941 or 1942 it might have picked up a tussle between two small children. Scarcely more than infants, one chubby little boy wrestled another against the new bull wire fence that was strung between the light, folded and crimped-edged, galvanised metal uprights. The two were scarcely taller than the chicken wire that was strung from the second or third top strand of bull-wire. The chubby little fellow, who was wearing a little topcoat, got the better of the other who then ran into the garden of the first house on the road. The swing of the five-barred gate was open. At that, the other little toughie ran away down the main road home. That was me. The other fellow was Paddy Redmond, and he became my first friend.

Five or six years on Paddy and I got enough long-line back to take twenty four hooks and made a mini-longline. Two old varnish or turpentine tins served as buoys – dwees we called them. In those days varnish, turps and floor stain came in tins with cone-shaped tops that were sealed with a wide cork bung, and made very serviceable floats. When we couldn't get enough lugworm to bait it with, we used snails, a lesson I had learned from Mr. Johnston, Uncle Bernie's friend. The most we ever caught was three fish, a place, a dab, and a bit of a codling. Going to school brought each of us other friends, and my going to secondary school further separated us. He grew to be a stronger man then I, and took Cecil Gilbert's place in the great rowing crew we had in the fifties. Our lives diverged then, and I met him latterly only once or twice at family funerals I travelled home for. It's only six weeks past that I heard he had died; something over a year ago; a hard death, I was told.

If Paddy was my first friend, Ronnie Tucker was surely the second. It came out of the friendship between my mother and Mrs Tucker that started I don't know when, but for certain before I was born, and lasted until my mother died about ten years ago. Mrs Tucker survived her by another eight years. Ronnie and I played with little plastic cars, that suddenly came on the market the Christmas after the war, in the log-pile at the back of Tucker's house. When we tired of them, we pretended to crash them, and anticipating Hollywood by twenty-five or thirty years had them burst into fire. Teddy Tucker, Ronnie's older brother, would then come racing up with the oil can, pretending to be a fire-brigade and pump oil onto the plastic toys that we had set ablaze with matches. It's a wonder we never burnt the shed down. The shed my father had hammered the 'galavanised' iron roof onto one Sunday morning, while Mrs Tucker appealed to him to do it quietly, as the people were going to Mass, and she herself would shortly be going to church. Teddy told me the story after I spoke at Fathers funeral, and told me also my fathers answer. I'm sorry, but it wasn't really delicate enough to repeat here.

Despite the bonfires we lit, and the spuds we cooked, and the divilment we got up to, and the Halloween nights we dressed up and went out together, Ronnie and I also went different ways in life, and I haven't met him for years. I didn't hear of his mother's death in time to go to the funeral. That's a thing I'm sorry for too.

There was quite a vicious little streak in me when I was young. I was known for my temper. I've always put it down to the fact that I was the third in the family, with four years between myself and Billy, and two between John and I. Billy and John were more of an age with the older fellows from the houses in St. Brigid's Terrace, and I'm certain that I tagged around after them. I therefore got more than my share of taunting. Naturally I lost my temper, and the more I lost it, the more I was teased. I was called 'Hitler and 'Spitfire', and, worst of all, baby or baby-face. At home I was taught to answer back "Sticks and stones may break my bones but names will never hurt me". But they did, and I preferred stones.

Greystones was a stone-throwing place, and we had plenty of them. I've been told of challenge 'matches' between the Blacklion gang and the Crow Abbey fellows, but was I never involved and don't really know if they ever took place. I do know that I left my mark on something like five fellows before I was seven. One who was running to escape after calling me baby, baby, baby, jumped onto a bench seat in front of the window of Stanley Carlyle's Anchor Café and taunted me that I couldn't get him there. I could, and I did. It's lucky however that my accuracy decreased with age, else I might have done someone a serious injury.

One day when I was in my early teens, I and a pal who worked as a messenger boy for my grandfather were challenged to a stone fight by Sean Dillon and another fellow whom I prefer not to name. Sean and the other fellow thought to use two great upturned concrete drainage pipes as forts and had prepared a stash of stones in each as ammunition. The messenger boy pal and I stood in the open on the edge of the road. Being mobile, we were the winners. By the grace of God only, no one was hurt, but the other two had flecks of blood on them, having been hit by splinters of stone that were chipped off the concrete pipes.

That same 'pal' and I were involved in another action about the same time. We had convinced ourselves that a lad named Paddy McGarry was an enemy and ambushed him shamefully just outside his front door. I punched him, once, savagely on the nose. Of all the things that I've done, this was the one I'm most ashamed of. I don't know if Paddy is alive or dead, but wherever he is, I ask his forgiveness. We had been friends earlier, when his parents came to live in Blacklion House, which was just across the road from 'Novara', the house I was born in. I think Blacklion House is still there, but not the great Beech tree that was in the front garden when we were growing up. Five or six branches had been cut off it at some stage, supposedly as part of an exorcism that became necessary when the house was haunted by the disturbed spirit of a person who hung himself – or herself, I don't know which -- from the tree. The name and the date were still carved into the bark, and legible when I was young. It was underneath it's great branches that I fought yet another pal, Liam Maguire, when I was only seven or eight.

The 'pal' and the 'other fellow' of the stone fight connected later when both were at sea on a Swedish vessel, and jumped ship together in South Africa. Some time later news percolated home that they had been jailed there for bank-robbery. When I was married first and living in Tanzania where I was a fisheries officer, I read in the local Tanzanian paper one day of a jailbreak in South Africa by two Irish bank robbers. They didn't name them. For me they didn't need to.

I don't remember what year the superb Walt Disney cartoon feature 'Pinochio' came out, but it must have been a long time ago: The son of the tailor whose brother walked my mother, used to call me 'Jimminy Cricket'. He was off by one character. The wilful little magically animated puppet who was always falling into trouble would have been closer to the mark. I made yet another friend with whom I fished and rowed, who showed me how to winkle big red eating crabs out of the crab-holes at the back of the pier, and around the rocks. He also showed me where most of the apple trees and orchards about the town were. I suppose its fair to say we taught each other lessons in robbing orchards, until one evening in the second year we were at this game my father asked me at teatime "Are you robbing apples? Of course I denied it vehemently, but my father went on to say that Guard Carroll had told him to warn me not to go near a certain garden that evening. It happened that this was exactly where we had planned to go. I turned my back on crime that night. Both of us did.

I only robbed apples one other year afterwards. The year my mother and father had to move to England and I was minding Eileen, Barney and Declan with Auntie Eileen. I had, still have, no remorse about that.

I had other, better friends. What we got up to caused grief to nobody. There was Leslie Spurling; he coached me and his younger brother Eric in manoeuvring the seven foot six inch punt his father built. Then there was David Robinson that I first travelled to England with; and Terence Evans, with whom I cycled to Silver Strand and to Brittas Bay and especially to his aunt and uncle who lived close to Rathnew. His aunt baked delicious brown bread scones, and we would have them hot from the oven for our tea with country butter and home made rhubarb jam. They had a prolific Victorian plum tree in their garden as well. I had pals of our own persuasion also; Seamie and Brendan Sweeney that I made camps with in the 'Bog' and the little bog – two swampy fields adjoining the circus field; and Sean and Kevin Dillon that became especially close friends after Sean and I joined the Gaelic League. That was later though.

It was interesting that although we fell into and out of friendship in Greystones in that time that we were growing up, I can recall no falling out ever over what religion we were.

It was different with the girls we were friends with. It's not that we fell out with them. It's more that we didn't fall in with them in the first place. We were divided off from them at the age of six or seven, not just in separate classes but separate schools, and didn't really get back together with them until most of us left school at the age of fourteen. Well, lets say from the age of eleven or twelve onwards. In the meantime we knew girls as sisters, and sisters of friends, rather than friends. Which was a pity. But that's the way things were. I've always had a problem with this because I aspired to something more open.

It's my ambition someday to be clever enough to query the causes and trace the answers from history as to how men and women divided themselves apart. The goddesses of Egyptian mythology, it is said, were more formidable than the male deities. The Romans

100

came to Ephesus and renewed the cult of Artemis, an ancient goddess of plenty, and left with the revolutionary new religion of Christianity. Their women had property and owned slaves equally with men – so long as they were high born. Their influence surely prevailed over our older Celtic culture. But the influence of women in Irish society is palpable. I have no doubt that the seeds of all that we complained of in this century were sown in the last, and however sown, were nurtured there. The hands that rocked the cradles were our grandmothers and our great-grandmothers. Not a man nor a woman but had a woman behind him or her. This century's feminism has now transferred the sodality from the church to the clubhouse, but the prospect of women opening up more to men seems to me no more likely with the one than with the other. Would it were different. I hope our daughters and our sons make it so.

I had no problem making friends with older people. Whether the age difference cancelled any potential for conflict, I couldn't really say, though at this stage of my life, I find the reverse age balance makes younger people's company enjoyable; which is a kind of confirmation. But the chance connection with one particular older person, Jimmy Smullen, developed into perhaps the deepest friendship in my life.

I had taken to going down to Billy Kinsella's house on Sunday afternoons after dinner at home. Billy and I were great pals, cousins once removed, and although he was really my Mother's first cousin, he was only about three or four years older than I. Billy was the younger of two brothers in a family of seven sisters, only one of whom, Terry, was younger than Billy. The older sisters were sophisticated working girls and all single with the exception of Kitty, the oldest, who had married a Dublin Solicitor. On Sundays the boyfriends would arrive to the house in cars, and after a late lunch, frequently play cards. Jimmy Smullen was friendly with Michael Kinsella, Billy's older brother and occasionally dropped in on Sundays also. That was how we got to know one another. I guess I was fifteen or sixteen at the time, by now into fishing during the summer, and that was just something else for Jimmy Smullen to get interested in.

The old rowing boat, the 'Kathleen', was showing its age. Each year the leaks in the rented garboard and bilge strakes got worse, and although they tightened when we 'sank' the boat, would open again when it dried out on the slip. Even the bitumastic paint I used one year couldn't cure it, although the colourful paint job one fine sunny day caught the eye of a Bord Failte photographer who centred it in a snap of the Sugarloaf taken across the boat-slip. Jimmy Smullen suggested we could replace the garboards and the bilge strakes, and this we proceeded to do. When we were at it we put a new transom into it also – it was cut from a broad elm plank that Jimmy got in Colliers the undertakers in Bray – and we renewed almost all the steamed oak ribs. At the start we knew nothing about boat building. By the time we were finished we were middling experts, and close friends.

Over the years the friendship continued to develop. When Georgie Ryan and Joe Naylor came down from Bray in Georgie's fine seventeen footer with half a dozen trammel nets that they shot on the Marl ground out off the Clyda Hotel, and hauled twelve or fifteen stone of fine plaice under our noses, we got into trammel nets. Jimmy Smullen and Georgie Ryan worked with one another in Morris's wallpaper factory in Bray, and so Jimmy and I got the inside track. We got a new sixteen-foot boat – John Spurling who had promised to build a boat for my father, built it for us – a couple of trammels, and a second hand four horsepower Anzani outboard which we bought from Georgie. Sean Dillon who had shared the experience of Charlie Hemp's story-telling with me in 1950, who had luckily survived our stone-fight unhurt, and with whom I was one of the Ceile organisers of the local branch of the Gaelic League, came with me to fish the nets. Within another couple of years Sean had finished a hotel management course, had married and moved

102

away, and his brother Kevin had taken his place as first mate. And Jimmy Smullen, too had married his girl friend Peggy.

Chapter Sixteen - John II, Verses 35, 36

I made other friends. My brother Billy had joined the Gaelic League in Bray where there was a very lively branch, and my mother thought that if I joined it would help with my Irish at school. I think I was thirteen at the time, and had already sat the Inter Cert. once. This was something the Christian Brothers in Synge St. did with the 'A' class at the time; let us sit the Inter in both third and fourth years, the first year for practice. At any rate, over that winter I found myself on the bus for Bray every Tuesday evening with the thruppence or so that I needed for the session and the same again for a bag of chips from the Lido café while waiting for the bus home. The following year a branch of the Connradh – the League – was started in Greystones, but it was organised as an "Irish Class" and I would have none of it. I had enough classes at school. But a couple of years later I was invited to their Christmas party and I fell into going after that. It was then that I fell in particularly with Sean Dillon.

There was a special quality to the people who made up the membership of the Bray branch of the Gaelic League at that time. People like Eamonn de Buitlear and Diarmuid Breathnach. Eamonn became famous as a musician, broadcaster, filmmaker and naturalist. Diarmuid, who went on to work in the National library, conceived the 'On This Day' formula and presented his marvellous vignettes daily on Radio Eireann until it seemed as if every newspaper and Radio station in the world copied him. It was Diarmuids sister, Cait who first told me about the Fleadh Cheoil, one day when we happened to sit together on a bus from Dublin to Bray. When the first Fleadh Cheoil was held, in Ennis in Co. Clare, she had wanted to go, but was nervous of doing so on her own. Eventually, quite late on the Friday or Saturday – I don't remember which she said – she took a bus out to Palmerstown and started hitching. Nervous she clearly was, noticeable even in her narrative, but she told me she would not have missed it for the world.

We were not as intellectual in the Greystones branch as that older group in Bray, but we took to ceile dancing with a swing. Sean Dillon and I became the main organisers of the ceile's along with Sean Brosnan who was at Synge Street School with me. A year or so after the Leaving Cert., Sean Brosnan still couldn't get a job at home and went to England. Brendan Kelly joined us then, and Sean Dillon's brother Kevin, and we became a tight little caucus dedicated to organising the ceili's. Fifty posters were as many as we could afford for any Ceile, which we ran every five or six weeks in St Killians Hall, and we had these made up for us in a printers somewhat to the back of the Technical School in Bray. Posting them became therefore a loaves and fishes job that took Sean Dillon and I, with occasionally Brendan Kelly and Kevin, on bicycles across the hill of Windgates to the Vevay in Bray, then out by Boghall to the Wexford Road which we followed past Kilmacanoge and Smiths of the Glen – the Glen of the Downs, that is – through the Willow Grove and Kilpedder until we turned at Newtownmountkennedy for Newcastle. We came back the coast road then by Kilcoole and Killincarrig cross-roads, making a short detour to Delgany – that's if we had any poster or energy left.

In the couple of years before I joined the Greystones branch of the Connradh, the band booked to play at the occasional Ceile was the marvellous Gorey Ceile band – all Murphy's and cousins. We invariably got the Carrickbrennan Ceile band, whose leader was a man named Piarais O Greagain, a spare kind of man with a half-military type of a moustache. Now for those who wouldn't know otherwise, Carrickbrennan is along the road that runs from Monkstown a block or two, as might be said in America, at the back of Dunlaoghaire's main street. Years later, while taking a bottle of beer in Hughie Joe's bar in the Radharc an Eargail hotel in Gweedore on my way home from work – this was when I lived in Falcarragh in Co. Donegal – I overheard a young woman in conversation at another table. Something in her accent intrigued me, and excusing my forwardness I asked her if she came from Crumlin or Kimmage or Drimnagh – all suburbs of Dublin's Southside and that I wasn't greatly familiar with.

"No" she said, "I'm from Dunlaoghaire". On the instant, I answered her "But you're not from Dunlaoghaire, you're from Carrickbrennan" and she was. Her accent might as well have been Piarais O Greagain's echoing down the years.

Breda Reynolds, was the girl who provided the music for us on the piano, at the weekly branch meetings, or classes, as we knew them. A lovely girl with a beautiful demeanour and an attractive, quiet way of laughing. It was with her in mind that I climbed the high wall of Captain de Kongs orchard out towards Kilquade, along with Sean Dillon, every Christmas to get mistletoe for the party. But she held me always gently at arms length. Nevertheless I cherish memories of walking her and a visitor, Marie Kennedy, who used come on summer holidays, on many a balmy evening from the harbour to her house on the main street. She was one of those friends I regret being separated from by life.

Breda had a younger brother, Seamus, who also came to the classes and the Ceiles, who boasted too much on one occasion of how discriminating he was. Particularly in regard to girlfriends. Challenged at a Ceile about a very nice girl from Bray he was known to be sweet on, he responded by demanding, "Prove it". We set out to do just that. As well as getting posters printed for the Ceiles, we also ran off handbills on a small Adana printing press that Father Fennelly, the parish priest, had bought for the hall. We concocted the idea that for the next Ceile we would add a hand-written invitation and inveigled Seamus into writing out some of these. He suspected nothing, because we had half the fellows in the class doing them as well. Armed with a sample of his handwriting, and the colour of ink in his pen, I composed a letter, a sloothery besotted bit of a love-y letter and forged it in his handwriting. Stamped and forged the post-mark on the envelope also. Smudged it with scent and perfume, opened it and crumpled it. We even, I think, applied a little lipstick. I cannot adequately convey the taunting that went on at the next Ceile, but when eventually he was allowed to snatch the envelope at the end of the evening and read the letter, he went bananas and had to be physically restrained from murder. The letter was flittered into shreds and scattered about the street, and we dived to retrieve them as if they were real, and to be treasured. He said days afterwards, that he knew he didn't write it, but the hand-writing was so like his own, he thought he must have done so.

It was forging of a different kind that I learned a little of in 1954/55, the year I attempted first Chemical Engineering at U.C.D. An old Ironmaster who instructed us in workshop practice demonstrated forge-welding, in which two bars of iron are heated almost to melting point – care must be taken not to let the metal burn – and may then be welded by hammering them together. I saw a blacksmith in an old forge out by the Pretty Bush where my father went to school use the very technique to make up an anchor for me. The forge had no electricity and the anchor therefore could not be electro-welded. Friendships, I believe, are formed something like that. Parts of our personas are cunningly hammered by events onto receptors in the personas of others, and vice-versa. The ultimate will be when we die. Like the carbon atoms that glow white hot in the surrounding plasma of a candle's flame, our souls will be consumed in what may appear to us to be an instant, but in the ultimate reality may extend beyond a million years.

Eugene Doyle was another Greystones Gaelic League man that became a special friend when we reconnected in first year at UCD. He was doing Civil Engineering. That was the year we first went to the great festival Ceiles in the Mansion House in Dublin. At that time the great conical ceiling of the Round Room was still draped with dark-green-and-gold velvet. Our first Ceile there was 'Fleadh an Oireachtais' and we were fascinated with the printed dance programme which listed every set and dance from nine till two. At one stage we misread 'Cór Ceitinn' (Keating Choir) as 'Cor Ceitinn' (Keating's Reel) and danced with the choir singers of the Keating branch of the Gaelic League immediately before they were due on stage; much to the disgust of the choirmaster who glowered at us all night. We were more au-fait at the Christmas ceile, 'Siamsa na Nollag', and at 'Fleadh na Feile' on the following St Patrick's day. By then we had come to expect the marvellous displays by the dancers of the Keating branch of special sets devised by their dancing teacher Matty O'Meleady. But on that St. Patrick's night a couple of five or six year olds, who literally flew over the floor, stole the show. Not till 'Riverdance' did I see their equal.

The only connection between Eugene Doyle and George Duffy was that both enjoyed Ceiles, both were friends of mine, and both bought motorcycles. They were the only motorcycles I ever had a go on myself. I came off both of them and I gave up motorcycling. George and his mother, who was widowed and who had an interest in Duffys Drapery in Thomas St. in Dublin, had only come to live in the area in the nineteen fifties. I met George when he came to our Ceiles and travelled in and out of Dublin on the bus with him when I was working with the Irish Glass Bottle Company. We were both interested in design; and in things Irish and things National. Things International also.In the aftermath of the invasion of Hungary in 1956 all sorts of functions were organised in support of the Red Cross relief effort. The Greystones branch of the Connradh organised a ceile. The parish priest of Kilquade, who had just finished a huge hall in Newtownmountkennedy, all built by local voluntary labour, held a gala-opening dance featuring Johnny Devlin and his orchestra. There was even a ceile in Roundwood. I don't remember now how everybody got there, but George and I, and some of the other Greystones fellows made it in Andy Harmon's five-hundredweight van. A Ford. What else? We had additional passengers on the way home. There were thirteen of us, and I was at the bottom, deliciously sat upon by a lovely redheaded girl named Eileen King from the Boghall Road in Bray. Those who know the 'long hill' between Roundwood and Kilmacanoge will appreciate just how good were those old Ford five hundredweight vans.

George, Andy Harman and I had a near miss in the same van on one later memorable occasion. We were on our way back from the Mansion House after Fleadh Na Feile on St. Patrick's night. It must have been 1957. Our dates for the evening were Cora Brennan and Ann Sheeran, two Greystones girls, and we had all enjoyed ourselves immensely. We even cruised around Stephen's Green a bit afterwards looking for a café to get a cup of coffee. By the time we were clearing Bray on our way home we were more than passing tired, and going up the convent hill we all fell asleep. I don't remember if it was Cora or I who woke and shouted, but we avoided disaster only by milli-seconds.

When it came to locally run Ceiles in our part of the world in the middle-fifties, however, one name stood out above all the others; Lewy O'Rourke. Lewy was from Bray, and had been to Presentation College, as had been Sean and Kevin Dillon, and Eugene Doyle. It was the connection with them at school that took him out to our ceiles in the first place. Once he got hooked he became virtually a one man promoter, and inspired the revival of the Gaelic league in Bray, when it had died suddenly after that earlier membership practically all went to university. As soon as the branch in Bray was functional, Lewy extended his attention to Enniskerry; and having met there Richard and Ann Fitzsimons whose father was Dublin Corporation's Water superintendent at Roundwood Reservoir, was inspiration for the Roundwood Ceiles also. And Lewy became my friend as well.

1957 was an ominous year from the start. In the aftermath of the invasion of Suez, petrol rationing had been introduced in Ireland. I applied for and was allocated a certain number of coupons for the outboard motor on the strength of the 16' boat being registered. The petrol for Andy Harmon's van for going to the Ceiles was bought with them. In the North, an IRA campaign got under way with five actions and one aborted, on the night of the twelfth, morning of the thirteenth of December, 1956. Clann na Poblachta pulled the plug on the coalition government. Doctor MacCartan, who was a member of Clann na Poblachta, and was also honorary president of our branch of the Gaelic League, told us how Sean McBride made the proposal to do so to the party. "Know you what you are doing" he said "You are putting yourselves out of office. You are putting in a Fianna Fail government. And you are bringing in the Special Power's Act." In the week in which I went to London in June with the vague idea that I might get well-paid work there, and might be able to help my mother to stay at home, twenty seven people were picked up by the Special Branch on Glencree bog and were imprisoned without charge in Mountjoy jail. The 'Wicklow People' named the twenty-seven. One of the names was George Gavan Duffy. Another was Seamus O h-Aodha.

The similarity of Seamus O h-Aodha's name to the Irish version of my own – Seamus O h-Aodain – convinced a whole heap of local people, including the postman, that I was in the 'Joy' along with George. Then when I came back from London, nothing would persuade them other than that I was too important to the 'organisation' and had escaped by having superior 'intelligence'. I had in fact started to think that George was getting involved with Sinn Fein – I think he was recruited after the St. Patrick Day's Ceile in the Mansion House – but by the time I got back from London, my mother's move had become inevitable, and this disturbed me much more. Even so, I was concerned for George, and for his mother, and I continued to call to the house, and often played cards late into the night with her.

It was a time to have friends, and I was lucky in having so many. Even luckier, I made two more during that summer. Pat Twamley who worked with Dublin Corporation, and his wife, Joan Dalton who was in light entertainment in Radio Eireann, had come to live in

Greystones, and were customers of my mother. Part of the deal on the sale of the business provided that we would rent Bobby Mooney's bungalow – it was he that had bought the stock and the goodwill – which was just across the road from the Twamleys, who seemed to take it on themselves to look out for Auntie Eileen and myself, and particularly for the kids. Both of them were into seafood, and I'm sure I kept them well supplied with crabs.

When I eventually took Auntie Eileen, young Eileen, Barney and Declan to England early in December, and came back immediately myself, it was Mrs Duffy who put me up. George had been released from Mountjoy on compassionate grounds long before that. She managed to keep me until January, until she could no longer afford to. Her money came three times a year only, and cash or the lack of it was a perpetual crisis. Over those next years, I was fed in Dillons, and in O'Rourkes, and Twamleys, and accommodated even with a bed for the night when I needed one. But those that I owe most to were my Aunt May who put me up without question when I turned back from Brighton in 1958; and Jimmy Smullen and his wife Peggy whose home became my home whenever I needed it until I left Greystones for good in 1964.

Verses 35 and 36 of John, chapter 11 says, "Jesus wept. The Jews therefore said, see how he loved him". I cried when Jimmy Smullen died. It had only been a few years since I learned how much older than I he was. Sixteen years.

Chapter Seventeen – The Man Who Invented the Skateboard and Other Cousins

I used to day dream about running down the field in which the great ventilator shaft for the big tunnel stood, holding over my head a miniature glider-like construction, that would lift-off, fly over the hedge at the bottom, and come to rest again somewhere down the next field. It was ignorance, and fear of the consequences, that prevented me from realising the dream. The odd thing was I believed so deeply that it was possible that in my imagination I could see myself soaring high over the old railway and the rampart wall in the 'Burrow', out across the sea to crash and drown somewhere about four humps off. Even if it should fail. My worst scenario was of rising off the ground, clearing the hedge, then slamming down in a tangle of broken spars and struts and limbs; in pain! I had a fear of pain.

Earlier, at school in Synge Street, I used draw on the squared pages of my science notebook a rocket shape with two deep stubby wings set far back, with an engine pod out towards the end of each wing. The original concept wasn't really my own; I had borrowed it from Sean Brosnan, who himself might have taken it over from Tommy Davidson. But I stood years afterwards in the Museum of Flight, at Boeing field outside Seattle in the USA, and put my hand on the realisation of that simple fantasy that we doodled at school; the 'Blackbird'! Ultimately built to the orders of the CIA, it flew so high and so fast that no Russian defence missile could strike it down. Control of its two great J58 Pratt & Whitney by-pass jet engines involved the manipulation of two cones; each set in the air-intake of one of the giant engine nacelles. The plane literally 'surfed' on the shock wave created just aft of the apex of each cone. I don't believe a more fantastical plane has ever been built.

In the same museum there was also a hang-glider on display. What price our imagination?

No disrespect to the man who first laminated and rounded the ends of a short plywood plank, and fixed two sets of skate wheels onto it, but the man who invented the first skateboard was Billy Kinsella. I know, because I sat on it, and scooted down the concrete path outside 'Sharavogue', the house just across the road from St. Killian's Hall. There is quite a steep hill at that part of Trafalgar Road. We therefore built up quite a turn of speed by the time we ran off the path where it turned along the front of Bayswater Terrace, and we usually ended by ploughing into the grassy triangle in the middle of the road; if we were lucky enough to miss running into the pillar-box.

This grassy triangle, where we pulled up the 'Shamrock' – the racing skiff – and turned it upside down to black-lead and polish the bottom before heading away to the regattas, was just across the harbour road from the crab wall. Below the crab wall were the fishermen's huts, and stretching from them all across the top of the beach to Stanley Carlyles 'Anchor Café' was a rough piece of grassy ground. At one point on the edge of this piece of ground, just in off the side of the road, was a small mound with a few heavy links of chain protruding from it. We never really knew what the chain was there for but presumed it had something to do with mooring schooners in the old days. Derek Ferns ran smack into this mound on a pair of skates one evening and looked fit to have killed himself, but somehow or other didn't. The skates suffered however, or at least one of them did. It must have been the other one that Billy Kinsella had the idea to sit the small triangular well-board from the stern of the 'Elsie' on it, and off we went skate-boarding. It never caught on though. Fingers wrapped over the edge to the underside of the board, to hold our backsides in position, were too vulnerable to sudden amputation.

Billy and I went back a long way. Both of us loved primroses, and would be off up the fields, even in February, searching the sheltery spots along the banks of the streams that seemed to run along the edge of almost every second or third field. That was when he lived in Blacklion, before the family moved to a little cottage named 'St. Annes', near the railway arch. The best primroses – the biggest, that is – were to be found in Pat Darcy's fields, or along the banks of the stream that flowed down through Massey's land in Redford. That's where the best violets were also. We seldom went to Massey's for primroses however; more usually it was for conkers in the autumn, but I passed it by daily on my way to get a fresh pint from the evening's milking for Barney. When he was a baby.

My mother had faith in Massey's milk and had got it all during the war, poured out into pint or a half-pint measures by Billy Smith, Masseys milkman, with the traditional 'tilly' thrown in every time for good luck. By the time Barney came along however, the Lucan Dairy had started daily deliveries of bottled, pasteurised milk and Barney's pint was a special order. I even made the run to collect it in the great blizzard in February in 1949, though I couldn't ride the bike on the way home. I could only push it through the deepening slush – six or eight inches as I recall it – and had to stop frequently for a slug of the still-warm milk from the billycan. Barney got scarcely half a bottleful of it that evening.

Billy Kinsella and I were out in the great snow of two years earlier; four weeks after it first fell; for sport. I had been sent over the road on an errand to get a newspaper – the 'Independent' – and met up with Paddy Redmond. It can only have been about twenty to nine in the morning, but the sun was already shining from a clear blue sky. The snow had re-frozen overnight – usually by late afternoon, when we got out of school, it would have softened – and Paddy and I decided to go sleighing on the sheet of galvanised iron that by then was a permanent 'fixture' in the field beside my uncle Johnny McKenzie's shop. At the top of Jink's hill. We were already sleighing down the bank nearest the road of the hollow at the top of the field when Billy Kinsella joined us. One might almost say up and down it. Because the surface of the snow was so icy, we were flying up the opposite side of the hollow such was our speed down the near side of it.

"Wouldn't it be great to go down the big hill?" some one of us asked. The two others were instant in their reply; and in chorus. "But who'll go in front?" The trouble with the big hill, which took up most of the other half of the field, was that it ended in a broad swampy pool at the foot of a giant alder tree. The sledges, as we called them, were usually therefore pointed towards the ditch, and this was a thick tangle of briars and blackthorn. We had no sooner sat on the sheet of tin than it shot off with so great an acceleration it frightened the daylights out of me. I had a momentary vision of my face being lacerated to shreds, so I struck one heel down into the snow. We took off on the instant; bodies and galvanised iron tumbled over one another. It was a miracle only that we weren't real, decapitated bodies.

When Billy got married – he and his brother Michael married two sisters – he went to live and work in England, somewhere about Coventry. After I got back from East Africa, married and with two children myself, I used to by-pass Coventry on the ring road heading for my mothers', from Winsford in Cheshire where we then lived. I never made the time to call in. I'm sorry about that. I could have done with more of Billy's sense of fun in my life.

Louie Hayden was another cousin that had a great sense of fun; when she was younger. As she grew up, life added burdens to her and shaped her character differently to what it might have been. She has often spoken to me about how much she regretted not getting more of an education; of how an education would have given her the confidence to write her story. But I have her permission to write a bit of it. I first remember Louie from a time when she was in the thatched cottage that is still there on the Delgany side of Killincarrig cross roads. That must have been after 1942. We climbed out of the little attic window in the gable somehow and made our way up the field and into the next, which ran along the top end of Devereux's Cherry Orchard. That was where the big swing was. Apart from the tea-garden, and the big purply-black juicy cherries themselves, this was always a great attraction, and it was common to see three up on it at a time; one sitting, and two standing facing one another. I'm sure I've even seen four – two sitting face to face, one in the lap of the other, with two standing – or five even. But Louie has earlier memories – she's older than I – of us going down to Ludlow's, when we were visiting Grandfather Hayden in Delgany, to get lucky bags. Just as Father and Aunt Eileen as infants in petticoats had done almost four decades earlier. Fan Donohoe told me how they would plead with the 'Boss' at the butchers stall until he gave them a penny or a ha'penny each. They would then call 'Shep' and 'Flo', two sheepdogs that spent the hours resting outside the shop, climb on the back of the dogs and say 'Lu'lows'. Whereupon the dogs took off, as precisely programmed as any computer.

There was another day, in the forties, when a whole assembly of Hayden cousins took off on a kind of afternoon safari to the Downs. Louie, Brian, Billy, John, Dermot and I. I don't remember if Brendan and Kathleen were also with us; maybe not, they might have been too small. It was summertime because the buckle came off one of my sandals, somewhere about the 'dogs gates' – the entrance to Delgany Golf Club – on the way, and I slither-slopped for the rest of the afternoon. We eventually made our way into the grounds of 'Silversprings' on the say-so of Louie that there was a swimming pool in the grounds that we could use. Silversprings is a fine house set in a beautifully landscaped sylvan surround near the village of the Downs.

True enough, there was a swimming pool there, separated from a half-round lily pond by an ornamental bridge, over, which we crossed. Beyond it was a fine mansion – Georgian or Victorian; at the time I wouldn't even have known the meaning of the words – with a broad flight of steps leading up to a fine hall door. We tested the water, and although I was dubious about how cold it was, and about having no togs, I was young and gullible enough to believe Louie when she assured me the lady of the house had swim suits and towels for us. All I had to do was go up the steps and ring the bell. I was halfway up the steps, and the rest halfway to the gate, when the door opened and a man came out – the butler maybe, I didn't wait to ask. Realising the others had fled shrieking with laughter, I took after them with my one buckle-free sandalled foot half-slithering along and half-hopping over the ground, in a vain effort to catch up. Every so often I had to stop to tighten my foot into the sandal, and to look about to see if there was a stone big enough to throw after them. Unfortunately there wasn't.

I think it must have been 1945 when 'John Hinds' came to stop with uncle Bernie in the house at Castle Villas just across the road from the Cherry Orchard, where old Mr. Devereux employed him. His real name was Gunter Heinen, and he had escaped from a prisoner-of-war camp somewhere in Britain. He is credited locally with influencing the Devereux's in setting up glass houses in which they grew tomatoes and chrysanthemums, but he stayed only about six months. Enquiries were being made about him, and he moved on, eventually making his way to the United States by stowing away on a liner at Cobh. I didn't really know about this at the time but was generally aware that Louie and Uncle Bernie travelled out to Germany in 1948, and that Louie was to marry the German fellow that had worked in the Cherry Orchard.

But it never happened.

By the end of January in 1958 things were getting very precarious for me. I was trying to sell vacuum cleaners door to door in Drogheda and wasn't very good at it. The particular machine was German-made, gimmicky, low-powered but surprisingly effective, and over-priced. It was called a Vac-master, and the company had at the very start of the fifties overturned the dominance of Hoover and

Electrolux on the Irish market. They achieved this by a policy of aggressive door to door selling and by setting up their own credit-sale agreement at a time when hire-purchase was severely restricted. '58 in Drogheda was different. The comparative boom of 48-50 had collapsed into the abyss of depression of 53-57, and Drogheda, that had measured its prosperity by the amount of over-time in the cement factory, had changed. If scarce money had to be spent, it would be spent on something they really wanted. A TV set. Only those working in the margarine factory had spending money. They were on over-time. It was among them I made the one sale a week that kept body and soul together for me. Even so I had to resort to putting in the two pounds deposit myself as long as I got a signature on the form, and this cut my commission from five pounds to three. It had to end.

I lodged the last three weekends at 170 Botanic Road when Mrs Duffy, George's Mother, could no longer afford to put me up, then baled out for England on the evening of my twenty-first birthday. Even if it had to be in England, home was hard to beat. I got a job as a railway porter. With British Railways. The pay wasn't great – seven pounds a week – but there was overtime, and after three months in the job, privileged fares at pittance prices, even for journeys to Ireland. I stuck it long enough to get a cheap weekend ticket home, then quit, thinking to go to Brighton to get hotel work for the Summer and save enough to go to Brussels for the 1958 World Fair. I already had my passport. Afterwards? Afterwards I would walk the world.

Work was scarce in Brighton. In fact I didn't find any that first day. "Come back in three or four weeks" they said at the labour exchange, "It's too early in the season yet". I retreated to a café to get a bite to eat, and to think out what I would do. The waiter, who was young – only a year or two older than myself -- was more encouraging. "You just need a day or two to look around" he said, "I could put you up for a couple of nights". The 'put you up' turned out to be a shared bed, and when he climbed on top of me in the middle of the night and gave me a blow-job, I figured it was time to get out of there. Naïve isn't the word for what I was at that time – I never even knew such a thing was possible. I tried Eastbourne, but when that looked as if it was where all the elderly English went to die, I turned back to London, got on the Irish Mail at Euston, and didn't stop until I landed in my Aunt May's in Killincarrig. "Can you put me up?" I asked, and took whatever answer she made as a yes.

Louie was married by then, to an Englishman named Bert Shippley, and they had two children, Noel and Maurya. They lived in Cricklewood. Brian and Dermot were married also, Brian to a dark-haired local girl named Annie Doyle from Windgates, and Dermot to a Scottish girl named Barbara from a place called Old Meldrum, near Ellon in Aberdeenshire. Only Brendan was still at home, and Alan. I guess we all knew Alan was Louie's child, but as it was no concern of ours we never thought to ask. We just took delight in his good looks – because he was a very pretty child – and his good nature; and let it matter little to us that he was black. Some others reacted differently at the time, as I found out the day of his funeral just a couple of years ago. He had died from uncontrollable bleeding following an operation that was too long delayed, on a tumour on his spine. At the funeral a boyhood friend of his, Jack Clarke, introduced himself and told how he used to defend Alan when other children threw stones at him on his way home from school; told me also how Alan and he marvelled at me vaulting the five-bar gate – I could take it straight, tucking my legs between my hands even from the lower level of the path inside the entrance – at the front of Aunt Mays. Its funny, Alan himself had said the same thing to me at some other family funeral only a few years previously.

During those few months I stopped with Aunt May, a sister of hers, Rose Bradshaw, came to visit. Rose was glad of the company, particularly as their brother, Hughie Bradshaw, had only recently died. They talked particularly of an episode during the 'Troubles'

119

when Hughie chanced upon the seduction of a young girl up the glen. She had been picking fraughans and the young man had suggested "The higher you go, the sweeter the fruit". Hughie, who was on his way into Delgany at the time, chanced upon the 'Republican' policeman and related what he had just seen. He took the story with him to consult Bernie who was in charge of the butcher stall that particular Saturday, the 'Boss' Hayden, my grandfather, being away. It was decided that the young man be arrested – such a thing could not be countenanced in the 'new' Ireland – and the republican policeman was despatched on that errand. And the young man was tried that night.

A trestle table was borrowed from the Forester's Hall and set up in a hayloft in the slaughterhouse yard. A fearsome looking Webley Revolver, and the Granny Reilly's family bible – my brother Billy has it yet – were laid out on the table as symbols of authority. It was Bernie himself who told me this later. He apparently had been appointed a 'Republican' judge. A tribunal of five was nominated that night and the young man was brought before them to face the witnesses; Hughie Bradshaw, and the republican policeman who gave evidence of arrest. The tribunal decided he was guilty. It was then that Bernie realised the burden of passing sentence was his, and wasn't at all easy. He proposed that there were only two sentences they could impose; shoot him; or banish him from the county. And shooting was too drastic.

Fan Donohoe, father's godmother, filled out much of the rest of the story. Not only was the young man to be banished from the county, but he was to be paraded outside mass with an account of his crime and punishment by the republican policeman on Sunday morning. Mass in the village was celebrated in the chapel of the Carmelite convent, the gate to which was just up the street from the butcher's shop. She told me how she and my grandmother stood at the hall-door of the shop and watched the goings on. She told also of the republican policeman being mortified, as most people took him to be the culprit.

On the Monday morning the young man was gone; not from the county though. He went into the RIC in Bray and reported everything. On Tuesday morning the authorities swooped, and lifted thirteen. A fourteenth name was struck off the list when my grandmother pleaded for Bernie – that he was only a young lad of seventeen, and in any case was away at work in the local power-station where he was indentured as an electrician. The thirteen, and the witness against them, who by now was starting to get very scared, were taken to the Bridewell in Dublin where they were to be charged. Thoroughly afraid by this stage, the fellow who had unwittingly caused the whole thing, now said he could identify no one; it had been too dark in the hayloft; it was lit only by a penny candle – and he didn't know anybody in any case. They were all discharged. But as they left the Bridewell, they were taken by the 'Tans' and interred in Ballykinlar for the duration of the troubles.

I know little about the end of this story; neither Bernie nor Father ever told me the names of the two young people at the innocent centre of all this business; and Fan Donohoe certainly didn't. But their lives were altered forever. He was shunned in Ballykinlar, is said to have gone into decline, and died in the thirties. She joined a convent and lived to the midfifties. Ar dheis De go raibh a n-anamacha.

I learned rather more about the ending of the Gunter Heinen story. Should you ever see the British film about Franz Von Werra, you will now know that he wasn't the only "One that got away".

John Hinds, to give him his proper pseudonym, got to the 'States' by stowing away at Cobh, and got out of the 'States' by stowing away in New York. It was aboard one of the 'Queens' – either the liner 'Queen Mary', or the liner 'Queen Elizabeth'. Word of his probable presence on board was radioed to the ship and the vessel was hove-to off Lands End. For nineteen hours. They searched from stem to stern but all they found was a bundle of his clothes on deck, as if he had gone over the side in an attempt to swim for it. Throughout it all he was in hiding in a ventilator, and stayed there all the time the vessel was docked in Southampton, emerging only at night when the ship had reached Cherbourg, its final port of call. Louie, and Bernie, certainly went to visit him in Germany in 1948 – she has always spoken of being engaged to him – but whether it was John Hinds she was in love with, and not Gunter Heinen, I have no way of knowing; and I'm not going to ask her.

I did ask her once about the story, when I visited her at her home in Cricklewood a couple of years after I first heard it from Brendan. Bert, Louie's husband, was at work. Noel and Maurya, her children, were either at school or in bed; Bert worked shifts, and it could well have been in the evening. I was hoping to learn a little more about what had happened. I wasn't disappointed. "He got captured again when he was in America" said Louie "and was being taken on a train to New York to be shipped back to the British". "But he escaped, and jumped off the train" she continued "and got away again". "He wrote to me to tell me" "Look, I'll show you the letter". And some sixteen years after the event, during which time she had a love child, had emigrated, had married and had two beautiful children; she went straight to her handbag to show me the letter from her 'one that got away'.

There were other cousins; John and Edwin McKenzie – Eddie played for a while for Fulham - an outer ring of Donohoes, McDonaghs, and Breslins on the one side, and Kinsellas, Whistons and Manweillers on the other; and the Haydens of Three Trout. It was years before I learned that there had been some family difference in a previous generation, and I had moved away before I had any chance of knowing them. There was Uncle Mick's family; Ollie, Derry, Ray and Lily. Apart from the time uncle Mick died, I can remember meeting Lily only once, although I had been in the little cottage in the square of Delgany as a child. She had the story of how her mother's parents' elopement led to her mother being born in India; led also to her grandmother being dis-inherited; but it is Lily's story to tell, should she choose to.

Billy Hayden – our Billy, that is - has researched the family tree, and I'm urging him to write his story. But for now, I hope the younger circle of relations whom I don't even know at all, that are rippling out, new rings entirely in the pond, may find themselves at the other side of a hedge as Brendan Hayden and I did. It seems Joe Murphy's cows had got into Mrs O'Reilly's garden and had eaten all her flowers, and Joe was getting the edge of Mrs Reilly's tongue. Joe was a local character, famous for his colourful turn of phrase, and he and his brother Frank grazed about fifteen head of milking cows on the long acre – the side of the road. Joe took the day shift, and sold the milk; Frank took the night shift. The cattle were always tended – accompanied – so they couldn't easily be prosecuted; though that was attempted more than once. Charlie Gubbins tried a prosecution for trespass, but I don't think even that succeeded; you couldn't blame cattle for finding the gate to a field open. Neither did Joe's response to Mrs Reilly that morning leave any comeback "Ah, I was wondering at the milk being so sweet lately, Ma'am".

Chapter Eighteen – Scholarship Boys

I was walking up out of Redford graveyard when I saw Paddy Donohoe just inside the gate. I took it to be his wife that was with him, and they were talking to my brother Billy. "Oh Jimmy": my brother said, "You know Paddy Donohoe", "Of course" said I. At that, Billy excused himself and moved away to talk to someone else at the funeral. Now I don't think it was Auntie Eileen's funeral, it was too recent; and I don't think it was as far back as my Mothers; so it must have been Kitty Kinsella's funeral – Kitty Ryan to give her married name. It wasn't Paddy Donoghoe's wife, but Willie Doyle's – he was also in the company – and she introduced herself as Gertie. "My maiden name was Flynn", she said. "You would be a sister of Tom Flynn's," I said, more as a question than as a statement of fact, but when she agreed, I was immediate with my next response. "Tom Flynn was the first of the scholarship boys", and I could see that this pleased her no end.

No one in the town had ever won a scholarship to secondary school until after the Christian Brothers came in 1941 to take over teaching the boys. Catholic boys, that is. Children from Church of Ireland, Presbyterian or Methodist families went to the 'National School', which we knew simply as the Protestant School. Before the brothers came, all Catholic children were taught by nuns of the Holy Faith Congregation whose convent adjoined the church grounds at the back of my Grandfather's and Sam Fern's shops. After first year, the boys were segregated out and attended the older national school in Blacklion, and it was this school that was taken over by the Irish Christian Brothers. There were three Brothers at first, Brother Buckley, Brother Kiniary and Brother Lannigan, who was the Principal. Brother Kiniary was replaced early on by Brother McInerney, and later on, they were joined by a Brother Kelly, who seemed to be semi-retired. Brother's McInerney and Buckley were both into sport, especially Brother McInerney, and all our budding footballers learned from him. One, Tommy Hamilton, who came out to the school from Bray, went on to play for Manchester United and the Republic of Ireland, and later on for Shamrock Rovers. What ever about Tommy Hamilton or Michael Woods who went on to be a government minister and with whom I then shared a desk, I have no doubt Brother McInerney influenced me for life. It was his class I went into when I came first from the convent. Learning our spellings was the hardest part of our homework, and for the first six weeks I got the strap every morning for not knowing them. This was despite the fact I learnt them every night. After that I gave up studying at home, and merely looked at them before class in the morning – and I knew them. Never afterwards was I able to study at home. That was the year my mother made the white bread and blackberry jam.

The next to get scholarships were my brother Billy and Jimmy Whiston who lived in Ennis's Lane, along with Johnny Duggan from Bray. That was 1945. And that was the way I always remembered it. But Breda Reynolds corrected me, gently as ever. Her older brother, Michael - universally known as Mockey - won a scholarship in 1944. They were followed in 1946 by Kieran Condell, Joe Mulcahy, and I think Willie Earles. That was a double hat trick, because they all were pupils of Blacklion School. At that time, Wicklow County Council allocated three scholarships yearly for boys for the whole county, and three for girls. The next year again Wicklow Co. Council awarded a fourth scholarship for the boys, all four going to boys from the Brother's school at Blacklion. The lads were John Hayden, Joey Murphy, Barlow Whiston and Jimmy Martin. And the next year again, the year I sat the exam, the number increased to five. I scraped through, along with, I think, Michael Spellman on two supplementary scholarships, while the full scholarships were taken by Kieran Spellman, Jim Brennan and Sean Brosnan. That same year, girls from Greystones Holy Faith Convent school took all three of the girls scholarships. The following year, the result was even better, with four scholarships going to Holy Faith pupils and I think five again going to the brothers. It couldn't last. After that, pupils from the two schools at Greystones were restricted to six scholarships in total, with another six being allocated to the rest of the county.

All the Brothers were moved on in turn, but I met Brother Buckley some years later when he came back on holiday to the town. He said that never before, or since, had he come across children with such a hunger for education as the Greystones fellows. The Brothers in Synge Street CBS in Dublin said something similar.

Not all of the Greystones fellows went to Synge Street – some went to Westland Row, and one or two to O'Connell's, while the Spellmans went to Colaiste Mhuire – but the bulk of them did. It was my brother Billy who had picked it, because Synge Street was so near Harcourt Street station and the rest of us just followed suit. It too was a remarkable school, and produced its own share of notables; Eamonn Andrews; Dermot Ryan; Richie Ryan; Gay Byrne; Shay Timmons, founding Managing Director of Ergas; Kieran Hickey, film director. But when afterwards we met senior Brothers Bill O'Leary, or the extraordinarily innocent Brother Ryle, it was the liveliness of the Greystones fellows that they remarked upon.

I think myself they identified correctly the thing that was special about us. We had a liveliness born of the freedom that was allowed us as youngsters; and although we were all classed as Greystones fellows, really we weren't. It was virtually only the fellows from the Barracks – Marine Terrace – along with some others about the town who were from Greystones proper. The rest of us were from Blacklion, Redford, Windgates and Ennis's Lane in the one direction, and Lower Kindlestown, Crow Abbey, Killincarrig and Delgany in the other, with a few from Kilcoole and the Willow Grove, and maybe a dozen and a half from Bray. It could have been a recipe for destructive rivalry, but somehow or other we avoided that. There was plenty of competition – with so many youngsters it would have been extraordinary if there wasn't – but because the

126

Brothers dispensed their discipline so even-handedly, there was a great sense that we were all equal; at least in school.

Things changed a bit when Brother Lannigan moved to the Mother House at Mount Sion in Waterford, and was replaced as Principal by a Brother Aherne. I guess he felt he had much to live up to, so he picked certain lads and made a special scholarship class of them. They were put sitting in the front desks where they could be given priority attention, and were brought back for extra tuition in the evening. I was one of those selected that first year Brother Aherne was Principal in Greystones, but I can assure you we got it no easier for being chosen. Rather the opposite. While Brother McInerney may occasionally have used a bit of a sally rod on days when he was not in good form, and while Brother Murphy who replaced him wielded the longest thickest baton I was ever hit with, the man who hammered me most was Brother Aherne – mostly with the strap, but often enough with the leg of a chair. His focus on us however may well have saved the other fellows because there is no doubt, that focus of special attention on the few discriminated against the majority. I had no trouble going along with being specially picked out then – the selection was made on the basis of class results – neither did I refuse the goose-eggs my Mother had Father bring home for my tea on the days he was slaughtering out at Cooldross for the 'Gent' Fox. They were to build me up for the exam. But when I just pipped Michael Barry to the scholarship by a margin of about ten marks in the history paper, I felt it a shame that he didn't get a scholarship also.

The I.N.T.O. – Irish National Teachers Organisation – adopted a very militant stance on scholarships, though I didn't know it then. In fact I didn't even know such an organisation existed, and would have had trouble even accepting that a teacher could be anyone other than a Brother or a Nun. But I learned something of it much, much later. By the end of the fifties chance had thrown a certain few of us into contact with lay national school teachers; young, lay, female national school teachers, straight out of Carysfort, who were teaching in the local convent school. Their particular attraction was not just that they were young, and new, and female, but that they had taken a flat in the town, and they threw parties. There was even a lay teacher in the Brother's school – in the new school that they had built on the Jink's Hill road. He was young also. His name was Pat Ryle, and he was a Kerryman. I took a great liking to him for his trenchant declaration that Killarney was not part of Kerry; he had been charged a tanner in it – six old pence – for a glass of tap water one hot Sunday afternoon when the county finals were played.

It was years before I met an older generation of teachers. In fact it wasn't until I had come to live in Donegal. I was married, with three children by that time, and, the oldest having already started school, got interested in things educational. The Principal of the local school was already past retiring age. One of his colleagues – himself a former principal from an outlying school that had been closed by the Department of Education in an amalgamation – was a member of the national executive of the I.N.T.O. at a time when the first Principal was expelled from the Union for giving extra tuition to scholarship candidates. Four or five years working and living in that part of Donegal, a place that became like home to me so readily was I accepted, gave me a glimpse of how things were, and an understanding of why individual teachers voluntarily gave of their time to boost the chances of pupils they felt had a chance. Gave me also an understanding, through contact with other teachers, of why they were so militant.It had not been all that many years since national school teachers were paid in arrears; a year in arrears!

Not long after the principal of that school retired, an I.N.T.O. dinner dance was held in Derrybeg, in Gweedore, at which three recently retired teachers were to be honoured. My wife and I decided to go, and I privately hoped the Principal I have been speaking of might be one of them. He was not. Whatever had happened, and howsoever it happened, had left a long echo. I will not name him now – that's for another story and another occasion – but I will remember him for our children, for the excellence of the educational start the first four of our children got in his school. And there were no scholarships involved. They had been abolished.

I once met the man who abolished the scholarships – effectively that is. He simply announced the extension of free secondary education to all pupils. Not that the level of fees charged by the Christian Brothers in Synge Street CBS in my time was excessive. I don't think it was as much even as six pounds a term in 1953 – the year I finished – and that itself was waived for some pupils whose parents had difficulty raising it.

It was ten years on from that, 1963 as I remember it, that I left Sligo to travel down the West Coast looking for a lobster boat. A company in Sligo, an offshoot of a major international food company, Liebigs Extract of Meat Co. – OXO – planned to back me in a crab-fishing development. I hitch-hiked to Galway and got a lift on one of the Aran Fifty foot seine netters, the Ros Guill, that was travelling back to Kilronan with the coffined remains of a dead islander for burial. That night I lodged with the Conneelys of the hotel in Kilmurvey, hauled trammels with them in a currach in the evening, and pots in their rather narrow-gutted half-decker in the morning; then got passage to Rosaveel on John O'Brien's Connemara hooker, and continued on my way to Dingle.

The boat I had come to see in Dingle was one of the first of the 32ft. class of transom-sterned half-deckers that were designed and built in the Bord Iascaigh Mara boat-yards. The boats of this class had all been named 'Bun –'; "Bun Brosna" for instance. But this particular one had been holed, sunk, salvaged, and renamed the 'St. Mary'. It was owned by a young go-getting contractor named Michael O'Sullivan who had a house just across from the pier. His man John, who was the one I think who had raised the wreck, and had stripped down and rebuilt the engine, tried his best to convince me of the quality of the work carried out on the vessel, after which we repaired across the road to Michael O'Sullivans house for a drink and to take the matter further. There were Waterford glasses everywhere, at least eight or nine of them – some business had obviously been discussed earlier – but fresh glasses were found while we discussed price, and how good a job had been done on the St. Mary, and other things. I didn't buy the vessel, which was a mistake because it was a bargain, but I was persuaded into going to the dance that was to be held that night in Benner's Hotel. Donough O'Malley would be there.

I met the man that night, and not much more. Anything political, and especially any local topic, was over my head, and I danced his wife three or five times while he was about his business. But when on that marvellous later occasion he announced free education for all, I knew who he was. And when he died at the unexpectedly early age of 47, I regretted his passing – few politicians leave after them anything like his achievement.

Few organisations achieve what the Irish Christian Brothers have achieved, and they are rightly credited with promoting an Irish, National, and Catholic consciousness. But we have focused too much on what they have done. So-called ordinary lay teachers from which grew not just the I.N.T.O., but the consciousness of of the rest of the nation, made their mark also. It too should be researched and written about.

Chapter Nineteen – White From End to End

If Georgie Ryan and Joe Naylor hadn't run out of petrol for the outboard motor, we might never have known about the run of plaice in the Marl. Not that the big longshaft Anzani – 4 horsepower – was sore on juice. But Georgie Ryan's seventeen footer was a deep, able boat that had been built to Georgie's own specification, and with the load of nets, men and fish they had on-board, might not just have made it back to Bray. For that reason they came into Greystones Harbour, and moored alongside the steps of the pier. We couldn't believe the amount of fish they had on board, nor indeed the pile of nets. Jimmy Smullen, who worked with Georgie Ryan in Morris's wallpaper factory in Bray, had told Sean Dillon and myself Georgie was getting plaice off the south beach in Greystones, but until we actually saw for ourselves we didn't really believe it.

Apart from draft netting, and a bit of drifting, the main fishing in Greystones was long lining. At the back-end of the summer, say the last two weeks in August, through September, perhaps into October, there was some years a useful codling fishing with trammel nets. The centre mesh in these was a four-inch mesh, but as the nets were made of cotton, these meshes usually shrank to something just over three and a half inches. I should explain that a trammel net is made up of three sheets of netting mounted together onto the one set of ropes. The centre sheet is of a mesh size that would just about catch the fish by the gills. Either side of that sheet are the 'walls'; sheets of large meshes, typically measuring either 18" or 24". Although dependent on the depth of the centre sheet, the walls would commonly be three and a half meshes deep of 24" meshes in a plaice net, and five and a half or six and a half meshes deep of 18" mesh, on the codling nets. They were originally a French invention, and work in a way that is 'tres diabolique'. Although the three sheets of netting are mounted onto the ropes in one common setting or ratio, the centre sheet is deeper than the outer 'walls'. When a fish swims into the net through one of the larger 'wall' meshes, the slack inner netting yields before it forming a 'pocket'. Feeling the restraint, the fish attempts a flip turn, and twists the pocket closed on itself. It may mesh or may not; that's immaterial, because it's already trapped. They are time-consuming to clear though.

At the time Georgie Ryan and Joe Naylor came to the pier, with their trammels 'white from end to end and two in every pocket,' there were few plaice trammels in Greystones. Jim Kinsella had four or five old nets. Jimmy Smullen and I had two; one that Jimmy knit from end to end using alder net needles we had fashioned ourselves, and one that we bought second-hand the previous year from Georgie Ryan along with a four horsepower British Anzani outboard motor. The long-line men had already gone to England, driven by the depression at home and enticed by the money to be made in a Britain that was desperately trying to rebuild after the 'War'. Bill and Thomas Doyle – Bill was more popularly known as 'Munger', but was not called this to his face – had a visit from Jack Phillips who travelled Ireland for Bridport Gundry Ltd. They were an old English Company from Bridport in Dorsetshire that made ropes, twines and netting. He quoted Bill seventeen pounds and ten shillings for a fifty-fathom trammel net with a 4 ½-inch inner, and 18" walls. But when the quotation was confirmed in writing a typing error reduced it to seven pounds ten shillings. I missed out on it, but I think a total of seven nets were ordered from the town, and the company honoured its written quotation of seven pounds ten shillings for all of them.

Those few summers leading up to the middle of the fifties were brilliant. The bed of plaice that George Ryan and Joe Naylor chanced on that first summer seemed to gather up every year in the one spot. We called it the 'Marl'. It was off the Clyda Hotel which was set back among some trees just off the South beach; a good half mile outside the town. The fish came in to feed on 'seed' mussel, which seemed to set yearly on stalks of seaweed that grew along beds of stones interspersed with the marl. We knew this because the

132

stomachs and guts of the fish were stuffed full with the crushed shells of baby mussel. And the flavour of the fish was out of this world.

With time, the extent of the bed became clearer; anything from seventy out to four hundred yards off the beach; nothing much north of the culvert – it was really necessary to 'open' the hotel itself before shooting away. To the south, the ground seemed to have plaice on it beyond the first black hut even as far as the 'Money' river. I walked the railway line on a recent visit, to check dates on the 'fishplates', and went away beyond the piles, which are no longer there; and looked also for the 'marker' for the wreck of the 'John Scott', a telephone pole with four stays, and it was no longer there. On the I way crossed the bit of a bridge over the Money River, and it was almost not there. It has been reduced to a trickle of a drain barely emerging from underneath one of the new golf courses that have consumed a landscape of fields, hills and hedges. Walking back to town I watched a dressed up Saturday morning golfer search for and then abandon on the railway line what I presumed to be a lost ball. Reaching the spot, immediately adjacent to the 'Money' drain, I paused to shake a chip of a stone out of my shoe and, spotting the errant yellow golf-ball, took the greatest delight in pegging it away out into the sea.

As one year followed another, plaice were found on grounds even further afield. John and James Whiston had a great shot one morning between the second black hut and the piles. This was an area where the direction of the flood tide when it made up, was at an angle to the flow of the ebb, not just the reverse, and nets shot in the area could easily get swept away by seaweed carried along by the current. The Whistons were doubly lucky. Others also; the Sweeneys, and I think, Jim and Mick Fields, shot nets away to the north, out wide in the 'Burrow', and took shots of fine big plaice. Jim Kinsella in the skiff – the Elsie – now shooting eight nets, covered the ground between the two black huts, but just in off the 'Ridge'. This was where my father rowed us in the 'Kathleen' with mackerel spinners and rubber eels to take golden kellick - a local variant of pollack. Here the nets took cod and pollack as well as plaice, but could just as easily deliver up a shot of dogfish. Sean Dillon and I hauled nets one morning that we had to leave over two days due to bad weather, and boarded seventy-two of the biggest spur- dogs I have ever seen. Nowadays, as rock salmon they would fetch the price of two new trammels. Then, we just dumped them at the back of the pier.

We observed that the fish were more active in the half-hour just before dark and in the very first hour of daylight, and took to shooting our nets before the dawn, and again in the evening. This was a change from our previous practice, so essential with long-lines, of fishing the slack of the ebb. There was a problem with 'marks' of course at night; Bray head, if visible at all, was just a black lump in the darkness; and even the Clyda hotel hid itself, as it were, in the barely discernible outline of the trees. We had to develop other skills; a feeling for the passage of time; an unconscious counting of strokes perhaps, when we were rowing; a sub-conscious processing of sounds and echoes in the stillness of the night; a total widening of our eyes as we scanned the darkness – I swear we even felt where we were with our skins - then a final pause as we either ceased rowing or stopped the outboard motor and "In the name of God" flung the leading buoy away into the darkness, and dropped the first anchor over the side almost before the buoy itself had splashed into the sea. Bare feet wide apart, one on the back seat, the other on a thwart – that was my style at any rate – we bent, grasped and threw the net away to port in a controlled frenzy. Leads for'ard, corks aft. Trammels and seines were overhauled into the well ready for shooting after the one fashion. In the 'Mac lir' as I shot the nets, Sean or Kevin, or on other occasions Leslie or Brendan or Eric, rowed away steadily, keeping the boat straight through the tide, until with one final shout of satisfaction the last buoy was fired away clear into the night.

It was normal for us then to go ashore on the South beach and pull the boat only just sufficiently clear of the water as was necessary; barely bow-on if the tide was falling; half a length clear if the tide was making. Then we waited for the dawn. I will never understand people who don't rise to see the morning, to see that daily renewal of the promise of life. Perhaps it's just an East Coast of Ireland thing with me. I have lived twenty seven years now on the west coast of Donegal, and the mornings come so often lashed with a rain that persists day-long only to fine away in the evening. On the East Coast, on the Irish Sea, the weather almost invariably fines away at night, so that the sea on fine summer mornings relaxes and is revealed in the first light of dawn as a liquid mirror. The base of the sky, at first a thick dark line that could well be only 2.8 nautical miles away – the horizons limit for a man standing at sea level – brightens into a band of distant cloud that could as easily be fifty miles. And when the sun appears, swelling from a sliver of a crimson line into a great red orb, in minutes only, it's as if this was that first morning, five million years ago, that man first stood up off the earth. That's how it was for us. An hour later perhaps, when we went off to haul the nets, a whisper of a day-breeze would be sending shivers across the surface. An hour, or an hour and a half later again, when we were already back in the harbour, nets cleared, and on our way home, a fine plaice or two hung on our fingers, others were only just on their way to work and we waved to them on their buses.

Breda Reynolds was one of those I waved to particularly; but there was never anything between us except friendship. She gently resisted anything more. Breda won a scholarship the year before I did – 1947 – and went to St David's secondary school. This had been started by the Holy Faith nuns in the most prominent of the big houses around the sea front. It was named St. David's, hence the name of the school, and had been a great mark for fishermen since it was built, sometime after the coming of the railway. In that half a handful of years after Georgie Ryan and Joe Naylor discovered the bed of plaice – rediscovered, really, because they had been there on

135

previous occasions – Breda, and Marie Kennedy who came on holidays, and others, were among those who strolled by the harbour to see the boats as we came late in the evening with our nets and our fish. And when the fish were either sold, or stowed away until the morning, we walked them home through the town, or around the seafront and across the footbridge over the railway. In two further summers, they were accompanied by two tall blonde sisters named Aherne, whose father owned the Palace Bar in Fleet Street in Dublin, and we did as much and no more with them also.

It wasn't all just seamless summer, however. Leaving Synge St. in 1953, an in-growing toenail that was stamped on by a school bully turned foul on me, and necessitated a three-week stay in hospital. Recuperation took longer. It was thirteen weeks before it healed. Hopeless job searching carried me into winter, and into a commercial school for a couple of months. There, I failed to learn touch typing – I concentrated too much on forming the letters and became conditioned to marshalling my thoughts at the same speed; another legacy of Brother McInerney – and have been frustrated all my life, knowing how but not managing to do it. A year at University followed. My mother paid the fees. First Chemical Engineering I tried, and failed. My brother Billy had done Civil Engineering, but got first class honours in his degree and was then working in the University. He was a particularly brilliant draughtsman, and I was afraid I wouldn't match up to him. In the event, it was the engineering drawing examination that I triumphed in, taking the highest marks ever achieved in first year – 192 ½ out of 200 – at University College Dublin; and failed maths, maths physics, and physics. I hadn't got the ability to study, and I lacked maturity; and I knew it. But how to tell my mother I didn't want to repeat? That was simple. Simple but not easy. I didn't.

I decided to do what Father was supposed to have done and run away to sea. I bought a fair-sized grip bag, packed as much as I needed, and headed off early one morning, leaving pyjamas and bed tossed, just as if I had gone fishing, and walked to Bray around the cliff walk to get the first train to Dunlaoghaire. This was all really to avoid being seen, because I had plenty of time in Dunlaoghaire to get a bite of breakfast before getting on the mailboat. It was a glorious morning. The sea was glassy calm, and as the ship cleared the bay and gathered speed, three deepening bow waves arrowed out astern on each side of the hull. Occasionally the spreading waves curled into a lip of foam that caused scattered guillemots and razorbills to dive ahead of the waves. Now and again the red and yellow beaks of puffins identified their owners long before we came up to them. There were more even than I had imagined there would be. I was just sitting there on one of the old wooden life rafts spaced about the boat-deck, enjoying the morning, when a voice interrupted my reverie. "Jemmy Hayden, isn't it? Well hello there, Jemmy". When I looked, I knew who it was, although I didn't know him at all well. A man from home. I think his first name was Jim – Jem as we said it locally – but I'm not sure, because he was always and ever known as 'The Bishop' Kane.

He was of an age that he could well have been at school with my father at the 'Pretty Bush', and he clearly knew well who I was. He was heading back to work in Birmingham, and I let-on that I was heading for London. Over a cup of tea, or maybe a bottle of stout, he declaimed at some considerable length that the day's youth hadn't the same spirit of adventure that their fathers had, and he thought this a terrible pity. We parted at Holyhead, he boarded the Birmingham train, and I headed for Liverpool, changing trains at Chester. I hoped somehow or other to get away to sea. But I didn't know how to go about it, and with my money melting away at thirty shillings a day, headed back to Holyhead on the offchance of a fishing berth. It was a Sunday afternoon and clearly chapel ruled Wales in those days: I couldn't get bed and breakfast anywhere. Sunday, you see. At ten o'clock at night, desperate, I tried the police station, and was given a cell, blankets, and much to my surprise, a decent breakfast; and was pointed in the direction of Llandudno.

I was lucky in Llandudno. A decent soul in the Labour Exchange wrote out a tab for a job in the St. George's Hotel as a dishwasher even though I hadn't got a permanent address. But it included bed and board, and the hotel as an address got round the regulation. There was the possibility also of a job as a porter, in a week's time, if Mr. Kemp, the Hall Porter, liked the look of me. It was the kind of thing that I needed more than I knew. When I was just finishing the first problem in my first exam – the engineering exam – at UCD, the supervisor, Frantisek S. Drechsler, who had been our lecturer in the Chemical Engineering faculty spotted my hesitance. I had just discovered I made a silly mistake in my nervousness, but had spotted a possible way to fudge it. Looking over my shoulder he saw what he took to be a correctly presented drawing, and pointedly but discretely gave me a quick nod. I didn't hesitate, but put French curve and pencil to paper and fudged it perfectly. Whenever after the Llandudno job I met at home with the 'Bishop' Kane, he never failed to comment on my adventuring and what he said about youth's lack of spirit. I could have gone through to Birmingham with him, he said. But he always seemed to admire my independence; and I continued to miss out on those who could put me right, could give me that quick nod.

One thing I didn't miss out on when I came home was a health problem I was born with. The tube from one of my kidneys went the wrong way around an artery and used to kink on me; and I can tell you it was painful. This was long before Magnetic Resonance Imaging was invented so the exact problem could not easily be diagnosed, and I was actually taken into hospital to have a gall-bladder removed. The common markers for gallstones were apparently, fair, fat, forty and female; and I was male, skinny and twenty. The specialist I was referred to was so convinced on the basis of a physical examination that I had gall-stones that he wrote to my own doctor – I read it upside down even as he was writing it – "an x-ray would only be of academic importance". But he was a top man and thorough and he organised tests and an x-ray: and he cancelled the operation, but only with half an hour to go. He came later into the hospital ward to show me the x-ray and to explain what he thought was amiss; and he apologised for his initial diagnosis. I never had a problem with the near miss, because what came through in everything that was done for me at the hospital, and in the visitors that came, was that I mattered as a person. It was years before I had the intelligence to realise that, but the important thing was that's how it was done.

I wasn't supposed to row, run, ride bicycles or dance that summer, in the aftermath of the operation. In the forty-eight hours after the surgery I dropped a stone and a half in weight and frightened the daylights out of all who came to see me. Eugene Doyle, my great pal from Uni and the big Mansion House Céilis didn't make it past the operating theatre. It was necessary to pass this on the way to the ward, and as Eugene came near to it, a patient was wheeled out with a bottle of blood on the drip. Eugene, who used to donate blood as long as his arm was screened off, went out like a light. Sean Dillon did make it; his diabetes sadly made hospital just too familiar. But as soon as I could walk down to the harbour, the nets came out of the hut, and Sean organised Kevin, his brother, into fishing with us. The longer the summer went on, the more I mended. There were days I drank six or seven pints of milk, but never less than four. I couldn't run, and did little rowing, but I went everywhere on Jimmy Smullens bicycle, and I never danced as much. Mostly with Eve Kelly; but I'll come to that.

Joe Sweeney is the one to talk to if you want to know about nylon trammel nets. He was the first in the world to order one. It was ordered off Jack Phillips from Bridport Gundry Ltd. I don't remember if it was 1956 or earlier. Joe had it a month before we even saw it. Anytime he came to shore it was hidden under the wellboard of the boat. What really flummoxed us was; where was he getting all the plaice; not just where? How? We even went out to sea and searched all the grounds looking for his buoys – dwees, we called them – but found nothing. Not until he took delivery of the second net did we find out. The two nets were just too bulky for the well, and had to be stowed above board.

Joe could have given lessons to many who had more schooling than him. He knew what it took me twenty-five years to find out; its no use going fishing unless you have the very best of gear. He had the advantage of our age group in being that much older, maybe four or five years, and while I know he was an allright guy to work alongside – I did two or three afternoons and evenings a week giving out change for Stanley Carlyles slot machines in 1950, when Joe was in charge of them – when it came to fishing it was every boat for itself. So it was; and the style that I developed was continually to explore for other, better pockets of fish; and if we were lucky for bigger fish. The biggest plaice we ever took in the trammels was one we hauled aboard the 'Mac lir' one particular day in 1956; what I thought would be my last real day fishing ever; the day before I started work in the Irish Glass Bottle Company. The fish weighed five and three quarter pounds, and I had supper, breakfast and dinner out of it. My brother Billy who was on holiday with us at the time with his wife Margaret cooked the other half-fillet for tea for the two of them. Do you wonder that this was somehow why I turned on my heel as it were in Eastbourne in 1958 and headed back for home?

Chapter Twenty – First and First in the Burney

What a length of time we were growing up, and yet how quickly we turned into adults. Billy was married at twenty- two, John at twenty-one. In spite of all the upheavals, Kathleen was married at nineteen, and I travelled overnight through to London from Galway and stood with my top-coat wrapped around me in John's flat off Brook Green while my sister-in-law, Jean, pressed my trousers, especially to be there for her and Eric. Eric was quite a bit older than her and worked in Canada on one of the Great Lakes ships. Duty became our companion at play, and duty is no fun because she wins too much. What? Do you cavil at my calling duty she? But she is! She can be male, but then she is called tyranny. Male or female, it wasn't duty that played 'pussy-fourcorners' with us infants in the concrete playground of the Holy Faith convent. We played it at the top end where the main stairwell of the convent butted into the yard, making a kind of a 'W' of the building, which was effectively wrapped about the playground. At the other end other children playing 'tip and tig' shrieked 'pax' as they jumped onto the little bench seats strung along the lunch shelter. In 'pax' they couldn't be touched. At our end, four of us occupied four corners of the alcove, one to a corner, while a fifth roamed the free ground in the middle. Pssh-wssh we would go, two of the corner holders beckoning to each other with curling fore-fingers, and creeping towards each other, then either dashing like mad for the other corner, or being forced back, while the one in the middle tried his best to capture a base. Or her best; we were gender neutral.

The other great game in the concrete yard was to crouch down on our hunkers and reach out our arms in front of us. Two others, one either side, took a hand in theirs; usually just by hooking bunched fingers into bunched fingers; then the two would race down the yard towing the one in the middle, taking sparks out of the concrete from the nails in our shoes. It was destructive both of the soles of our shoes, and the seats of our pants – if we crouched too much. Sister Mary

Anthony certainly said so one day she caught me under tow. "What will your mother say if you go home with holes in the soles of your lovely shoes?" she said, "That she has had to work so hard to pay for". The shoes were a simple pair of brown leather children's shoes that fastened with a single strap and a small round button of the kind that kept coming undone as the buttonhole stretched. But it wasn't Sister Anthony that put me off the scooting. It was the day I was pulled into a grey mess of cat sh--e. I have never taken to cats since.

Well that's not completely true. Any boy that ever read the Tarzan novels, and especially one who read not only everyone of the Tarzan books of Edgar Rice Burroughs, but his John Carter, 'Warlord of Mars' and his 'Princess of Venus' series, as well as his Hollywood-set thriller, and his Western 'Bandits of Hells Bend'; any boy I say, as I did, could not fail to glory in the great cats. And when 'Jeserich's circus came to town with an entire pride of lions and a magnificence of tigers, I was enthralled. I was an avid reader of 'Wide World' magazine which published only true accounts of peoples adventures and strange stories from Britain's colonial world, and remember being thrilled by a repeated article on 'The Lionmen of Ussure' – I think I have the title correct. This was more spine-chilling even than the Michael Douglas film 'The Ghost and the Darkness'. A story that seemed inexplicable except by linking the natural and the supernatural. Man into beast, and the reverse. Even today's transgenic experiments by the giant chemical internationals don't come near. Certainly unbelievable. All the same, there was a jaguar in a solitary cage in Chester zoo when my own children were growing up, whose coat in wintertime was just fashioned to be stroked; but the eyes ...!!

In the 'Brothers', tip and tig was more robust; our efforts to escape more vigorous; frantic even. The second and third year classes, taught by Brother McInerny, were located in the supper room of St. Killian's Hall, at the bottom of Trafalgar Rd. A rounded concrete wall marks the boundary to this day, enclosing a small gravelled area in front of the hall. The ground inside the wall is level, that on the path outside rising with the hill. In our efforts to get away from our 'tig' pursuers, we vaulted the wall, both on one hand and two. This game switched easily into vaulting competitions, which spread even to a similarly rounded wall skirting the harbour in front of Bayswater Terrace. This is where I acquired the skill that so fascinated Alan Hayden and his pal Jack Clarke. I could manage about five foot three straight on with no more than five steps of a run, by placing my two hands on the wall or gate, and tucking my legs between my arms as my feet cleared the top.

Apart from chasing, the principal game we played in the Brothers was 'taws' – marbles - but only in the spring of the year. Then the 'chalkers' and the 'bottlers' were brought out; old porcelain and bottle glass marbles respectively. The bottlers were seagreen in colour, and said to be cut from the crown of the dimple in the base of old wine bottles. There were glassers as well; new glass marbles with a rainbow spiral of colours twisted into them. The principal games were; shooting at a line of taws to try to knock them out of a ring, those knocked out being deemed won; and a following up kind of a game where the taws were shot along the side of the road. In both cases the marble was shot by a flick of the thumb from the crook of the forefinger. A timely thrust of the elbow could give it added velocity. In the game along the road, which had elements in it of the 'bools' that they play both in West Cork and throughout Northern Ireland, I think the taw was won when one player got three successive strikes on his opponents' marble.

One year, a new game started. Small, cheap – inferior – painted clay marbles were on sale in the shops. They were no good as 'strikers'. They weren't big enough. And even when we won them, we felt cheated; we didn't consider them equal in value. I don't know who invented the game, or imported it, but 'taws' were never really played with afterwards. It was a bit like what is now happening to us in the 'European Union'. This new game is somebody else's; theirs, not ours, and our older games have no more value. Back then even, we knew it for what it was. They weren't real 'taws', so we called them 'mebs'. And the game was different. Individual players pitched a single meb towards a bit of a hole that we scooped out of the ground with our fingers. The nearest to the hole then got first go at pitching all the mebs together. Those that went in the hole he kept, as well as all those he was able to shoot in with the crook of his forefinger. Then the next player, the one who was second nearest at the start, had his go; and so on. When one game was over, we all clamoured "First, and first in the burney". It was a forerunner for us of 'pitch and toss'; almost a 'Fás' course. But I didn't graduate that far either.

Eleven was a great age for me; I got to go out at night; provided my lessons were done of course. And they were done, on the train home from Harcourt St. That was after I won the scholarship. Being out at night really meant being allowed up to the 'top' of the road, where St. Brigid's Terrace T-d off the Blacklion Road. Facing the terrace was a bungalow with a pebble-dashed wall in front of it. I think it was Lawless's and between it and the next house, there was a street lamp. In 1948 there was simply no traffic to speak of, people walking or on bicycles, - a car was almost a rarity – and the road was ours. In inner city Dublin, in the side and the back streets where people lived, it always seemed to us there was a terrible scramble for existence. Every street was filled with cars and lorries and four-wheeled drays, with kids hop-schotchin' in numbered chalk squares marked out on the streets and the pavements. Urchins scutted on the backs of drays and lorries, and young-wans swung in a bight of rope around virtually every second lamp-post. We had the whole terrace to ourselves; for 'O'Grady says do this'; or 'Relievio'; or some other game that involved us running like mad and en masse from the fence at one side of the road to the safety of the fence at the other, to avoid being caught. Inevitably though we ended up playing 'Truth or Dare', all lined up along Lawless's wall and hoping that we would be dared to kiss Betty or Jean Redmond. Not only were they good looking, but they and Peggy Halliday, who had the added attraction of being a newcomer, were more grown-up than some of the other girls. Jean later married my brother John.

The year before I went to Synge St. my brothers John and Billy spent quite a lot on fireworks. It was money they had made during the summer fishing their first longline. They mostly bought them in Gearys, a toy and bicycle shop near the Grafton St. corner of St. Stephen's green, although fireworks were on sale in many other shops as well. They were things we had read about in comics, but hadn't really seen before the end of the war, and they were a great novelty. That particular year, Billy and John added their purchases to a general selection some of the other older lads from St. Brigid's Terrace had accumulated, and we were treated to a great fireworks display in Dessie Murphy's front garden. That's as I remember it.

Unfortunately that was just about the last year such a thing was possible. A disastrous fire in a family owned shop that sold fireworks in the city led to a complete ban on their sale, and that made an end of it. No more rockets or bangers. But just as prohibition in America failed to kill off people's thirst for liquor, a mere government ban couldn't end our fascination with fire and explosions.

I could well have been the model for Kipling's king of the monkeys in the 'Jungle Book', the one who was determined to learn Man's great secret – fire. Chastisements, and multiple warnings that those who play with fire get burnt, were of no avail. Indeed Billy Kinsella and I nearly invented blackened steaks long before Cajun cooking came on the scene, one time we had slashed our way into a thicket of furze bushes to make a camp. We hadn't anticipated how prickly it would be, and decided the easiest way to clear the thorns would be to burn them. We only just got out in time. Another few seconds and it would have been our asses on fire. Some of the other big lads at Blacklion Terrace – St. Brigid's – were themselves lucky not to have their tails scorched one day they wrapped a .303 bullet in a piece of newspaper and set fire to it to set the bullet off. Within moments, all you could see disappearing around the corners of houses were backsides and boot-heels as the lads realised before either Mrs Eddie Evans or Mrs Harris herself that the cigarette Mrs Harris was smoking as they filled their buckets at the pump had been cut in two by the flying bullet.

There was a simpler way of making a satisfying bang. Carbide lamps hadn't quite dropped out of use. Some old-timers still had them on their bicycles, and they were a feature of the one or two horsedrawn 'phaetons' – open carriages – that provided a taxi service from the station. The 'Cruise' Doyle was the last man to operate one. The carbide – calcium carbide – could be got in Allie Evan's bicycle and hardware shop. It was sold in small, tightly lidded tins. The lamps themselves, which were no longer on the market, were designed to drip water into a closed chamber containing the carbide. The resultant chemical reaction released acetylene gas, which was discharged through a jet in front of a reflector. This is where the lamp was lit. The banger was simpler. Nothing more than an old paint tin with a hole near the base. We dropped a piece of carbide into it, spat on it, stamped the lid tight, and held a match to the hole. No quicker way of getting a response. "Them wee feckers R– T– and J– H– again."

I had a worm of curiosity in me though, and had opened up bangers and rockets – factory-made fireworks – to see how they worked. Bangers were simply made; a tube within a tube, both filled with a fine free-flowing gunpowder mixture, the bottom end sealed with a plug of clay. The inner tube, which was about as fat as one of those metal slim-line ball-point pens, had glued about the top of it a scrap of blue touch-paper – tissue paper impregnated with saltpetre. The tubes themselves were made of light cardboard; scarcely more than rolled paper. When lit, the fuse paper merely glowed, but was obviously hot enough to ignite the gunpowder in the inner tube. This

146

burnt down to the centre of the main chamber where, propagating in all directions, it closed the first tube like a valve – and bang!

A rocket was simpler still, a solid plug of gunpowder. I'm not sure how they compressed it; it was almost as if the mixture was moulded into the rocket casing, and contrary to what you might expect there was no nozzle or restriction other than the casing. I experimented once and made up a rocket. 'Beg your pardon, I should first have told you I got into making up my own gunpowder, from sulphur, saltpetre and charcoal, and rolled up my own banger-casings from glued drawing paper. This is appropriately called cartridge paper. But for the rocket, I used the casing of a metal bicycle pump, and tamped the powder home as tightly, and as gingerly as I could with the head of a knitting needle. Because the powder was still somewhat loose, I screwed back the little restricting piece that made a seal for the plunger. For a rocket stick, I hopped on my bicycle and headed for Belvedere Hall. This was a fine house on the back road from Templecarrig to Windgates that few people were aware of. It was quite close to the ruins of Belmont House, which appeared to have been the second house of the Kilruddery Estate, but was on the opposite side of the road, and was well screened by high hedges. The reason for my interest in it was that the best bamboos in the neighbourhood grew at the bottom of the garden, and could be got at. One of them did fine duty as my rocket stick.

A westerly gale was blowing the night I set it off, and I had difficulty lighting the fuse paper. But I had put a good shake of gunpowder into the paper before I twisted it up, and managed to get a sheltery spot on the far side of the garage, so that the fuse and the powder fired up well. For quite a few seconds I thought it wasn't going to lift off at all – the whole apparatus was so substantial, I had pushed the stick deep into the clay to get it to stand up – but then it took off, well, like a rocket. I suppose it soared almost three hundred feet, I have no way of knowing, and then exploded with an unmerciful bang. My worries about the casing falling on somebody's roof were needless.

Just one other person saw my rocket. Sean Brosnan was heading into town to play billiards in St. Killian's Hall, and was taking the short cut along the railway line from Ennis Lane. I suppose he was the better part of a mile away. He said afterwards that it frightened the life out of him.

I only once made a better explosion. Sometime later the same year I buried a Brylcreem jar containing about half-a-pound of gunpowder in the back garden. Deep in the garden. I used the centre tube of the metal pump I used for my rocket as a fire-tube to get the charge even deeper, and had half another one leading the fire into the jar. I had tried smaller Brylcreem jars earlier – my father used lashings of it on his hair, and there was no shortage of jars – but the explosions didn't really satisfy me; they weren't loud enough, and they cost too much. I was frustrated. Too much effort for too little return. It was years before the fast-food restaurants coined the phrase 'double quarter-pounder', but let me tell you I was there before them. The charge was set at the far side of the garage – as usual – and once lit it burned for an age, without anything seeming to happen. So much so, I was advancing from my cover to investigate when it actually blew.

It was super. As good as the maroon, that was fired to call out the coastguard, any day. I was rooted to the spot. True to an ingrained habit of mine I started counting. Approaching thirty I heard the whistle of the fall-out coming from the sky. At thirty-two, it was as if half the gravel in the garden clattered on the galvanised iron roof of the landlord, Sam Evans' house, down at the back; simultaneously thrashing all his fruit trees. "What the ---- ?" The shout was even more startling than the explosion. Sam was up a ladder, picking apples I think, when he was shelled out of it. I didn't wait to find out what next. I was gone.

It was more than thirty years before my mother even mentioned that Sam spoke to her about it. One occasion that I was visiting my mother in Bushey. He thought it was the maroon, she said, and stopped what he was at to look down to Greystones for the second flash!

--------------- 0 ------------------------------- 0 ----------------

The fishermen, and those that were involved in the rowing, indulged in a more civilised 'pass-time' on the patch of dirt in front of the fishermen's huts atop the beach at the harbour. They played 'quates'. It should probably be spelled 'quoits', but as what they played bore no resemblance whatever to the kind of horizontal 'rings' that's played with grommets of rope, I'll stick with my phonetic spelling. Our game involved two players pitching two 'quates' each between two 'mottes', there being a 'motte' at each end of a ten-yard pitch. A 'motte' was just a large flat rock, anything up to about a stone in weight. 'Quates' were simply flat rounded stones from the nearby beach. Order of play was simply decided by each player pitching one quate to the further motte. Nearest man went first. Scoring favoured the man whose quate or quates was nearest the motte, each man pitching in turn. 'Two in' was classed as an ace, but only when the primary score was reached. We played for ten and two aces. A 'toucher' counted as two; a 'leaner' was three; and a 'rider' – quate ending up on top of the motte – five. The man who scored, pitched first on the return leg. Simple.

Play is not that simple however. Somebody always wants to introduce a scorecard. It's seemingly not enough that we do it ourselves. Billy Kinsella for instance was diagnosed as having a heart-murmur but was determined not to let that take from his life. He converted his bicycle into a fixed wheeler – this was widely regarded as making a bike faster because of the need to keep pedalling – and did the five and a half miles from the 'Tech' in Bray to his home near the railway arch in Greystones in twelve minutes.

For fun, and the achievement of it. Achievement was more the thing that drove me; mostly the achievement of keeping up with my two older brothers. No one knows the desperation with which I jumped daily off the train from Harcourt St. before it had stopped at Greystones railway station, raced to the bicycle shed, and pedalled furiously up the Church road, and then the Church Lane, only to be overtaken by my brother John on the corner at Blacklion school. One hundred yards from home. It was never declared a race, but it was. The chips gritted off my teeth, and the tears of frustration still glistening in my eyes as I came through the door could have told you that. I was eleven.

I don't know if I can adequately tell you how playing games has fitted me for life, or if indeed they have had any effect at all. I tend now to avoid head to head competition. Too many people want to write their own rules, to make it their game, not ours. And there is too much of it. But be warned, don't challenge me to a fight, or threaten me or mine. I still bite, scratch, scraub, claw and kick. Figuratively speaking of course. And throw stones. Home is like the bench in front of the lunch-shelter in the play-yard of the convent, onto which we jumped for 'pax'. I defend it against all-comers, and the taxman. But hey, who's for a game of quates? First and first in the Burney, anyone? I was never any good at 'taws' in any case.

Chapter Twenty one – Tell Whiskers there's Another Fine Salad on Deck

Its immaterial now which paper the ad was in, the 'Independent' or the 'Press', I answered it in any case and was called for interview. "Skipper Training Scheme" it was headed, and it called for four years fishing experience. This was the time I was stopping with my Aunt May. When I walked in on her straight from England and asked if I could stay, she had simply said, "of course, Jimmy" in a diffident kind of a way and nodded her assent. Over two months later, I knew myself something else had to happen for me, and soon. I had fished the couple of trammels with my cousin Brendan, but it wasn't really enough. No more had it been enough the year before when I was minding Eileen, Barney and Declan. It would be more than forty years before I knew that what I should have done then was buy six trammels from Jack Phillips. But where in 1957 or 1958 would I have got the half year's wages it would have taken to buy them?

The four years fishing time was a puzzle. How could I convince people that I had accumulated that much? Joe Naylor was one of those that helped me out. Jim Kinsella was another. I had got to know Joe on one of the occasions I was in hospital. He was a solid lump of a man with a red face that made him look as if he was a heavy drinker, which he absolutely was not. The man was a 'Pioneer' – a member of the Pioneer Total Abstinence Association. He had an accident. Working on a roofing job on the new Christian Brothers Secondary School in Stillorgan, a plank he was manoeuvring a wheelbarrow along slipped out from under him, and he and barrow fell through rafters, joists and ceiling. A table set for dinner broke his fall; and his pelvis, arm and leg; and that's how he came to be in hospital. When I needed it in '58 he gave the o.k. to write up a spell of sea-time on a substantial kind of a half-decker he was fishing; and what with that and Jim Kinsella's letter, and affidavits I swore out myself in front of a Commissioner of the

Peace, I documented just over four year's worth. That got me to the interview.

It took four to interview me. Me and the others, that is. The most important of the interviewers, although I didn't know it at the time, was a Mr. MacNamara. He was secretary of the Dept. of Fisheries. Another was named Paddy Kerrins. He became secretary of the Dept. after McNamara. I knew only one. That was Captain Freyne from the Dept. of Transport and Power. I knew him because it was usually he who came every three months to inspect and take out the 'Rocket Apparatus'. I should explain that there was a local volunteer coast-guard unit in Greystones that maintained and manned an apparatus for establishing a 'breeches buoy' lifesaving link from the shore to any vessel grounded and in distress offshore.

The whole apparatus, which depended on getting a line out to the vessel by rocket, was stowed on a cart, which would have taken one of the Budweiser Clydesdales to pull it, and this was kept in the Coastguard station. The volunteers were called out by the 'Maroon'. Now it wasn't just the fireworks, the rocket, and the maroon that was the attraction for me. We were paid half-a-crown – two shillings and sixpence - for volunteering; five shillings if we were 'members'. When we got cute we became members. Another half-a-crown for throwing the 'lead' the furthest. Jimmy Redmond usually won this. The man who went across in the breeches buoy, on the one in three practices that we actually fired the rocket from the road in front of the Grand Hotel, got ten shillings. This was usually Derek Ferns. He deserved every penny of it, being hauled from the top of the 'Rocket Pole' which was almost on the rocks out in front of the 'Carrig Eden Hotel', right across the cove to the bit of a cliff just in front of the 'Grand'.

The interview for the Skipper Training Scheme was a bit like being hauled across in the breeches buoy for me; a certain percentage fright, but to an even greater extent, a challenge. Captain Freyne,

152

who was Master in Sail and Steam, helped me more than he knew, because he asked questions that I had to think out answers to. Some I should have known, like the arcs covered by a ship's riding lights. Others I hadn't ever really thought through – what my ambitions were for instance – and I had to answer the questions on the run as it were. Even today I'm not ashamed of my responses: A bigger boat! How big? Forty-five feet! Maybe forty horsepower! But ultimately I'd like to get into marketing. That's where I felt the biggest challenge lay.

I was picked for the scheme, I think by the skin of my teeth. Somebody must have dropped out at the last minute and I was the most immediately available. A telegram was delivered on a Friday afternoon to my Aunt May's directing me to report to Cathal Brugha St. on Saturday morning for a medical and sight test; and to have my gear with me ready to go to sea. After the sight test, carried out I think by a Captain Quirke of the Dept. of Transport and Power, I was collected in a van driven by Paddy Kerrins. The others who were to go to sea with me, Dennis Daly from Cape Clear, Michael Canning from Barna, and Michael Doogan from Kincasslagh, when they were introduced, told me what Paddy Kerrins had said on the way from Cathal Brugha St. "Go easy on this next lad. He has a beard. He's a University type. We don't think he'll stick it."

If I were ever to give up, I should have given up that morning, there on Sir John Rogerson's Quay. At the very least, I should have jumped overboard as we passed the slip at Ringsend where I first raced in the 'Colleen Bawn'. But I did neither, whether through stubbornness, or determination. Desperation maybe. Going aboard, I was quickly inveigled into climbing the mast to reeve a fall for the radio aerial. None of the crew looked too capable of doing it just then. A figure, a blonde woman, quite beautiful really, dressed as if for Ascot, even to the hat, hailed me from the quayside. "How about it, whiskers". I had grown a beard ever since I started as a railway porter with British Railways earlier that year. I was slow. I was only just figuring out the howabout what, when Moriarty, whom I had only just met, told her very curtly to clear off, and was scorchingly abused for his troubles. Sean Moriarity – he once told me a Fleetwood Skipper came closest to the correct pronunciation of his name in a letter he addressed to Mr. Murray Artie – was the ship's husband; he was Operations Manager of BIM. A fellow called Frank Loughlin was his gopher. He was on the quay also. The woman? She was well known, but only as 'the gypsy'. I don't think anyone knew her real name.

Aboard the 'Loch Lorgan' - that was the name of the vessel – we were made known to the crew: Paddy Sugrue, the skipper. He was dark, lean and wild-eyed; a Valentia islander whom I always had difficulty understanding. I should have stuck with him for the next ten years, because I would have made money, even from whitefish. A young man, he was Irelands first fully ticketed skipper, and a much better fisherman than many other less able men gave him credit for. Big Billy Davis – Billy the blacksmith, or Billy one-eye, he was blown up in Milford Haven during the war – a Welshman, was the mate. Mick Lilburn, the bo'sun, was the man I took most to, and ended up being classed as his 'old china' or 'oul segocia!' I was to share a watch with him, and at night tempted his appetite with whiting sandwiches, the fillets coming from fish fresh off the deck and fried in butter with a shake of salt and pepper. But for now he was a stranger, and just as drunk as anyone else on deck.

The three 'Loch' boats, the 'Loch Laoi', the 'Loch Lein' and the 'Loch Lorgan' were bought out of Germany by 'An Bórd Iascaigh Mhara', the Irish Sea Fisheries Board, shortly after its inception at the start of the 1950's. The objective was to train Irish fishermen as deep-sea trawlermen in the tradition of the middle and distant-water steam trawling operated out of Hull, Fleetwood and Grimsby in England, and out of Granton and Aberdeen in Scotland. Paddy Sugrue, who crewed one of the vessels when they were taken originally from Germany across the North Sea and through the

154

Caledonian canal was the only one to gain his Skipper's full ticket in this programme. Crew for these ships came and went through the 1950's, skippers and mates from Fleetwood and Milford Haven, and Irish trawlermen from the World War one vintage ships 'Cosmo', 'Father O'Toole' and 'Father Damien' of the Dublin Steam Trawling Company that operated from the South quays. A McCabe family appear to have been involved in this company, and it links in my mind with a chain of fishmongers shops of that name that was later bought by M.&P. Hanlon; and with McCabes South City Market; but the history of this was from before my time.

Paddy Sugrue wasn't the only one I had difficulty understanding that first morning I joined the 'Loch Lorgan! Danny O'Leary from Castletownberehaven was equally unintelligible, but I put it down to the delay in getting away to sea. Both the Lighthouse Bar, and Kelly's had seven-thirty in the morning licences that seemed to account for the general state of all hands. Only the cook, a Manxman named Johnny Oliver, and the Dutch engineer, Michael Dykstra were fully sober, although I must admit Paddy Sugrue was fully in charge as we motored down the river. When a brawl broke out between Billy Davis, Mick Lilburn and Danny O'leary on the fore-deck, he wasn't long sorting it out.

The spectacle these older hard rough trawler-men made that day wasn't the only theatre worth watching. We trainees were worth a scan also. Minor actors in the drama, we too showed our character. Dennis Daly from Cape Clear, six foot three, broad as a door, ten years a first-class radio operator, around the world three times; he was the oldest, and the most polite. His roughest expression of exasperation was "Dear me, Jim". We shared digs in Galway afterwards, and he shamed me because he went on his knees every night to say his prayers. But he helped me get my ticket, in his own way. At the test, he wrote for me as I read the Morse lamp. But it was really he who was reading it; even with his back turned. I never could read, not even if my life depended on it. The next oldest, and equally experienced in his own way, was Mícheál Doogan from Kincasslagh. He had navvied in Scotland, and worked with other Donegal tunnellers in compressed air gangs in London. A blow out under the Thames had left him hard of hearing. He was cool though, and if he didn't stand back and pare tobacco for his pipe with a pocketknife that day, he acted as if he was doing so. I was wondering both how I had got into this predicament, and where I needed to jump to to get out of it, but the fourth man in our squad, Mícheál Canning from Barna, Lord have mercy on him, seemed as if he was only waiting his chance to jump in and take a snot at somebody. Mícheál and I became special friends, and after his too early death some years ago I wrote elements of our friendship into a short-story that was short-listed and broadcast in the first Francis McManus competition; how we ate our lobster-bait, and navigated into the Shannon with a sixpenny road-map.

Johnny Oliver was my nemesis. Nicknamed 'Handlebars' – he had a pure ginger RAF-type moustache – he had been apprenticed as a chef at the age of sixteen on the Isle of Man boats sailing between Douglas and Liverpool. Nursing a pint in a dockside pub one afternoon, he was picked up by an "old dear" – his account – and jumped ship. What with satisfying her at night, and spending the money she gave him on younger women during the day, he said he was as thin as a whippet by the by the time his father came to find him, boxed his ears, and put him back to sea. I'm not sure the father did the shipping companies any favour by doing this because, at the time I sailed with him, he had court cases pending against three shipping companies – I think Limerick Steamship Company, Wexford Steamship Company, and either Palgrave Murphy or Irish Shipping. There weren't exactly too many companies left, and that's why he had taken the berth on the 'Loch Lorgan'. He was a very good chef, like many other sea-cooks, but he had a seeming compulsion to always test the system. In the case of the 'Loch

Lorgan', he wanted to assert his right to take leave in accordance with the ships articles. I did as much myself on the 'Cu Feasa' two years later.

On the 'Lorgan', however, Johnny needed someone to take on the job of cook for a week or two, and over the first five weeks at sea I was the patsy being coddled up to take on the job. Every time he came aft from the galley, two or three dinners in one hand, and stood at the door of the mess-room to tell yet two more dirty jokes, he was somehow or other acting out how easy it was. Each time he did so he put our dinners at risk also. Both the 'Loch Laoi' and the 'Loch Lorgan' had been modified and re-engined to accommodate us 'trainee skippers'. The foc'sle had also been refitted and was, for the time, very comfortable. Back aft, it had been necessary to add on a new mess-room, hence the need to come aft along the deck with the grub. For some reason, uneven ballasting of the fuel tanks perhaps, the Loch Lorgan usually steamed around with a noticeable list to starboard. And if the cook startled the gull that perched atop the mizzenmast, as he emerged with plates of dinner from the galley, the dinners were liable to be splattered instantly with hot seafood sauce.

As I said, I was soft-talked for a solid five weeks. Now the five was important. We had been working 'half-landings', five days at sea followed by a night ashore, then another five days with two days ashore. A full trip was ten or eleven full days at sea, followed by two ashore. After our fifth half-landing, Paddy Sugrue, the skipper ordered the cook to take on grub for a full trip. Fishing in the Irish Sea was bad, and we were to go north to the Minch. Johnny Oliver's nose was immediately out of joint, and he straightaway protested our right to two nights ashore before a full trip. The argument continued again in the morning on the quayside until Moriarty's thin Kerry patience got the better of him and he snapped out to Johnny Oliver "Do you want two nights ashore?" "Yes" was the answer. Moriarty's in return was even quicker. "You had better throw your f----n bag ashore. And you can follow it". No prizes for guessing who went cook.

By and large I didn't make a bad fist of it. For one Sunday's dinner I even served up a steamed sultana pudding. I never made one in my life, but had often watched my mother doing so, and imitated her as best I could. The tradition on the steam-trawlers was that a heavy suet duff with custard was the Sunday special. I cooked mine on the Saturday night, tending the coal-fired range with my shoulder braced against the bulkhead while a full force eight gale raged. And I raged at 'Galway', Mícheál Canning, for crowding out the tiny galley as he got a 'heat'. Water got in on it – the pudding I mean – and it was somewhat over-cooked, but it went down well with the custard, and there were grudging concessions that maybe I might make a cook after all.

The concession lasted all of an afternoon. I had turned in – cook's privilege - intending to make a quick salad for tea when I rose. But when I went down the after-peak, where the vegetables were stowed, I could find no lettuce. There were however a couple of fine solid cabbages. I had read of cabbage salads, but you should remember this was long before coleslaw became the ubiquitous garnish it is today, and had no idea how such a salad should be dressed. Undaunted, I dished up a plain tea of finely chopped pale-green cabbage, quartered tomatoes, sliced onions and hardboiled eggs. Billy Davis, the mate, was the last to come for his tea, by which time all hands were primed, waiting for his reaction. The sprayed cabbage salad went clean over the side. "What the hell" "Bloody cabbage" "Whiskers!!" A trip or two later a bale of straw fell out on the deck when the cod-end strap was opened one morning. I can still hear Sugrues hoarse laugh that I heard then back aft even in the galley: "Tell whiskers there's a bloody fine salad on deck".

In April 1959 all seven of us got our Second Hand (Special) Certificates. Michael Doogan from Kincasslagh had bought a forty-

158

five footer, 'Realt Na Mara', from Scotland with a cousin of his, and had given up the course. Along with Dennis Daly, Mícheál Canning and myself, the other four who got their tickets, who had been to sea on the'Loch Laoi', were Gregory Conneely, Ciarán Gill, Jackie Campbell and Brian Crummey. Our tickets were the first issued from Dublin, and each of us afterwards believed we personally got the No.1 Certificate. No wonder. They were issued on April first 1959.

Chapter Twenty two - Kiss the Girls

All my life I have fallen for every young woman I have ever met and quite a few older ones. In fact I wanted to make love to all the women in the world, but lacking the opportunity and inhibited by the deep sense of right and wrong drilled into me along with my catechism at school, I stuck to the one. The fear of hell might have played a part in this temporary celibacy also; it was a big thing with Catholics in the fifties. Not that I associated women with hell. Then.

Much is made nowadays, in the militancy of this feminism-spiked world, of the s---s that men are, but if our tentative over-vest-bodice-and-jumper fumbling's constituted sexual oppression, never mind abuse, God help us all. We are programmed for this male thing, it is in our genes, and women should celebrate us for it and join us in the pleasure, purpose and fulfilment of life. For five million years we have clawed ourselves upright; fashioned clubs, spears, arrows and thought; and ventured far beyond the forest in our search for destiny. We are programmed for this also; continuously to explore; and if some day you find that we have come in and left our weapons aside, as the Esquimeaux hunters were seen to do by French missionaries, about the age of forty-five; take it as a sign that we are finished. But not before!

I suppose the first girl I ever fell in love with was Joyce Evans. She was the oldest of Jimmy Evans daughters and lived in the house next door. I suppose I was four or five, hardly six. She was older, I think not as old as Billy, but somehow older than John. My mother had invited her and her younger sister to one of our birthday parties - not mine - and I have been smitten ever since. For weeks afterwards I stood on my tip-toes and pushed the branches of the thin hedge on our side of the garden wall aside to peer down into their garden to see if I could get a glimpse of her. She was gorgeous. Alas, I think she was sent away to boarding school and although we continued to be next door neighbours, she faded out of my life forever.

The first real girlfriend I had was Eve Kelly but it was no sudden affair. I first saw her, I think, on the day I finished the Leaving Cert. Exam, getting into the train at Bray. We had earlier travelled out from Harcourt St., flittered the last of our copy-books out the window of the train as we crossed the viaduct between Carrickmines and Shankill, and had been up the town of Bray to get a sixpenny half and half wafer in the Silver Lounge. They had beautiful home made ice cream, and the half-and-half was part vanilla part strawberry made up into a 'slider'. Back at the station as we boarded the early afternoon train from Westland Row to Greystones, we spotted two young girls in Diocesan uniforms getting on the train. The girls of Diocesan College, which taught classes only up to Inter Cert., wore dark green blazers and short grey culottes – split skirts we called them - and were readily identifiable by their uniform. No other school in the city had either green or such a combination. One of the two girls, Jean Sloan, we knew already because she had been coming on holidays to Greystones for a number of years. The other was immediately noticeable because she had fine blonde hair, cut short, kept neatly in place with an Alice band. More than that, really. She was short, snub-nosed, had a personality that beamed readily from a face prone to laughter, and was all of thirteen years old. Fourteen at most. Her breasts were no more than buds. When we got to know her later Noel Furlong rather cruelly named her 'Buttons'. But in a town where nicknames were the norm our use of them defused their cruelty in most cases, and our affection for the people named eventually led us back to using their proper given names.

I think Eve came again the following year, little changed in either height or dress, but I can't be sure if I'm expanding one year's memory into two. We were snapped a couple of times together in photographs later published by Valentines as postcards; me in a gabardine, trousers tucked into my socks, holding a bicycle; Eve standing alongside. We were at the head of the slip. It was a

161

favourite place to be, either sitting on the flat wall overlooking the beach, or leaning over the round-topped wall above the slip itself. It was here one day that she confided to Jim Brennan and I how worried she was that her parents might divorce. I couldn't say whether she had or had not any real cause to think they might, but for her at that time the worry seemed all too real. When a couple years later I met and got to know her mother, was it any wonder that her mother remarked that I might easily be ninety, not nineteen. I had perforce become counsellor and confidant.

It wasn't quite summer the following year when next I saw her. I was minding the shop for my mother one Sunday afternoon, and was weighing up half a pound of figroll biscuits for some visitor when a Morris Minor pulled up at the corner of the Church wall and a young girl got out and walked back into the shop. It was a blonde young girl, quite heavily made up, and her breasts were testing the very fabric of a tight, pale orange sweater. I was just in the act of pouring the figrolls from the scoop of the scales into an opened paper bag, and I missed by a mile. Only once did I ever do anything like that again. In 1964 I was working on the oil-search in the North Sea and was ashore in Middlesborough. One afternoon I was having a cup of coffee and a turkey sandwich. The café, which was called something like 'The Green Parrot' was most un-Middlesborough-like, and served sandwiches in a bun with prawn and turkey fillings and such. It was the beginning of the era of the mini-skirt. As I was about to tuck into my sandwich, a very fashionably dressed young woman – she looked like a model – came in, drew all eyes after her through the café, sat down and crossed her long legs one over the other all in one motion. I nearly bit the ball of my thumb right off.

Eve Kelly nearly did for me too, that summer of 1955. She hadn't come on holiday that year; only came one or two Sundays. One afternoon when a fellow named Ken was making a play for her, and the whole gang went for a swim across the harbour to the North Wall, I had no option but to follow suit. I was a poor swimmer, and had never swum as far in my life before. It nearly killed me. A boil I was getting on my chin developed into a fully-fledged carbuncle the following week it took so much out of me, but I got the girl on the day.

I got the girl all the following year, indeed for a year and a half afterwards, and we developed a deep and passionate friendship. Not so deep that we overstepped the mark for the time. We didn't jump into bed together. Sex was a thing we talked about but didn't do, although we snogged our faces off so much in the balcony of the Adelphi one night, we were put out by the assistant manager. Somebody complained. We couldn't object too strenuously; we were there on free tickets that Eve got for babysitting for the Manager himself. One night, when the conductor wouldn't take her on the last bus to Churchtown – he said it was too full – I walked her all the way from the city centre, then came back and climbed over the railings into Stephen's Green where I froze in a shelter for the rest of the night. I'll tell you this much, I think the need to catch the last bus did more for celibacy than half the urgent warnings from the clergy. Eve was a lovely person, and although it faded out for us, probably because she was Church of Ireland and I was Catholic, she has a small corner of me still. And I have so many more stories, but they're for a private occasion.

One evening in that same summer of 1955 that I swam across the harbour, Nessan O'Shea and Colm O'Reilly arrived one evening at the head of the slip with two girls in tow. Nessan and Colm were doing Chemical Engineering at UCD, which is where I got to know them. Sean Dillon and I had already hauled our nets – the fishing was slack – and had stowed the outboard away in the hut. Nessan and Colm had driven out of the city for the evening – Colm had the lend of a Morris Minor – and were interested in seeing this boat I had talked about; and I was interested in being introduced to these two good-looking girls that were with them. I only remember one of them now, Rita Dunn, who as it turned out had been at boarding school, at the Holy Faith Convent in Glasnevin with my sister Kathleen. "Hold on here a minute" I said to them, and ran over the road to get the outboard motor.

The fishermen's huts were set into the bank below the wall that bordered the road at that part of the harbour, and it took me no more than a couple of minutes to get the outboard from ours. With the tank full it weighed about three and a half stone, but I put it up on my shoulder, ran up the bank, jumped the wall – it was about two and a half feet high – fastened the outboard on the transom, pushed the boat down the slip, boarded the two fellows and the girls, shoved off, climbed over them to the stern, and started the outboard, all in one motion. I could never do it as well again, not even if Orson Welles himself were to direct it.

As Lewy O'Rourke got more and more involved with the revival of the Gaelic League in Bray, and its promotion in Enniskerry, and became the principal organiser of the Céilís in both places, my initial acquaintance with Rita Dunn grew into a very enjoyable friendship. Rita lived above the village of Enniskerry in a cottage at the edge of the grounds of the Summerhill Hotel. This was owned by a brother and sister of her father, who had died when she was younger. Her mother was a Kerry woman who worked as a telephonist in the central exchange in Dublin, and had one other daughter, Kathleen. Both Rita and Kathleen came to the Céilís, as did the Dillons, George Duffy, Brendan Kelly, and some of the others from the Gaelic League in Greystones. I can't remember which years exactly, but I can remember a special couple of parties, one in the Glencormac House Hotel – after it was bought from the Jameson family, it had been developed by Millie Kinsella's husband Harry McAnaney as a fashionable wateringhole – and one in the Summerhill Hotel itself. I think this must have been in 1958, the year I came back from England and asked my Aunt May to put me up. That was when I started calling on Rita Dunn, and I know it was I who organised the party in the Summerhill.

That was the year it all seemed to happen for me. Only a few years before I had once asked Kieran Condell how to talk to girls. He was certainly the handsomest fellow in Blacklion, and if you search out his picture in one of Derek Paines books of photographs you will see he had no problem in that department, where as I felt I had difficulties. But now it was different.

Two girls from Birmingham came on holidays to Greystones and Kevin Dillon and I got off our marks with them. Claire Watson and her friend Mary were from Bournville. On the first evening we walked up the north beach with them, Mary told Kevin that she intended to stay a spinster all her life, and before even he could make much of a response, added "Not physically, of course". It was really just a holiday thing, or so it seemed. Ten days of romance and more or less restrained passion. But Claire went home and talked of Jago this and Jago that, and a jockey named Brian Jago was posted for some race meeting simply as Jago. The horse came in at eight to one and Claire's father had a couple of pounds on it. She wrote to me, and it became more than just a holiday romance.

That same summer, two young teachers, Moya McGowan and Máire Niellan, and another girl they shared a flat with, threw a party in one of Connie Archer's flats at the far end of the Green Lane. Near the station. The other girl's name was Lena Fogarty. She worked either for Doctor MacCartan at Kilquade Sand Company, or in the office of the fertiliser factory at Woodstock. She was somewhat older than the other two. A fourth girl was also involved, again somewhat older than Moya and Máire. Her name was Lilian Feeney and she was teaching infants in an orphanage run by an order of nuns in Rathdrum. That was just about the first time I met her; at the party, I mean. I had been invited, along with Sean Dillon and I don't remember who else. It was a great party. I skoffed three whole apple tarts myself. The girls got well shot the following day just clearing the fruit from the bottom of the punch bowl – some Wicklow lads had reinforced it with half a bottle of vodka – and Lilian Feeney made me promise I'd write to her from Galway. I guess the party must have been in August or early September rather than summertime, because it was either at the end of September, or the beginning of October that we started our studies for the skipper's tickets in the Tech in Galway. My writing skills, that I developed a couple of years previously in letters to Eve Kelly, were about to be tested; all passion and romance for Clare Watson; more cerebral – no, that's not quite right – more depth of soul for Lilian.

I missed out with Rita Dunn, not just in serious romance – much as I wanted it, she already had a fella, Padraig McNally, and I felt it ungentlemanly to cut across him – but in the horse stakes also. The first evening I called to the house I came out the lane and down the road to the village. The next time, she showed me the short cut, the 'Beech Walk'. The next time I stayed almost too late, and had to take off like a mountain hare to catch the last bus to Bray, to connect with the last bus for Delgany (my stop was Killincarrig). As true as chickens lay eggs, on the next day after the one occasion a horse called 'Beech Walk' was running in the "Enniskerry Handicap Chase", and on the other, 'Must Fly' in the Delgany Plate. On both occasions I bought the paper too late to get a bet on; and they both won.

I don't often dwell on those days now, but when I do I think; I should have made love to them; at least to those who were especially close. I know I said it was a male thing, but its not, it's a people, a human thing. It's in all our genes, and there is no way in which we can give more physically to each other. But if I had done so, my life would have been totally different, and maybe that's not what was planned.

Chapter Twenty Three - J. Arthur Dixon Postcards.

She rejected my first letter, Lilian Feeney did. "If you're not going to write a real letter" she wrote "Don't bother writing at all ". So I guess I did write real letters, but what they were about I couldn't now say. They had to be about Galway, and about the docks and the Cladagh and Connemara; about the short dark-haired girl from Bohermore who taunted us with "Caithfhidh go bhfuil siad-san ag freastal ar an gCeard-Scoil", speaking about us rather than to us; and about Brendan O'Donnell who was agent for the swarthy Spanish fishermen who came intermittently to the docks, and who looked like a Spaniard himself. Born and reared on the spit of land between the old Commercial dock and the river, he learned his Spanish and his French, Breton too I think, on the very pier itself. Dennis Daly and I were introduced to him by Mícheál Canning on the very first night we came to Galway. He came staggering off a Spanish trawler, about as full of wine as it is possible to get and still almost stand. When next we met him, groomed, sober and meticulously dressed, we almost failed to recognise him.

Brendan was one of the most intelligent persons I ever met, and had a gleeful, almost wicked sense of humour. It was he who named Delia Lydon's pub 'Teach Baluba'. That was after the fishermen fell out with Mrs Freeney over grub bills and decided they would take their drinking custom elsewhere and they threw the travellers out of Delia Lydons. But that was still in the future, and for the moment Dennis and Mícheál and I just met Brendan from time to time on our forays about Galway.

We didn't forage all that much. Our wage as trainees when we were at sea was a pound a day, a mere ten shillings a day when we were ashore. Studying in Galway, we got four pounds a week. Our digs cost us three pounds seven shillings and sixpence, and what with half-a-crown for laundry, we were left with ten shillings apiece spending money. Don't ask me how we lived; we just did. When we were at sea we were regarded as being on wages and a deduction for a stamp was made; only because we were paid fortnightly, and because our fortnight cut across the boundaries of the Department of Social Welfare's deduction week, three week's stamps were stopped on us every time. When I protested the wrong of this to Frank Loughlin, the ship's husband, he retorted "that was the way it was always done". But I persisted, and when the over-deducted two and thruppences were all paid back to us, we had a 'big' week. Even so it was Dennis Daly, who had been a first class radio operator for ten years, who subsidised Mícheál and I by insisting so many times on picking up the tab for our coffee and cakes in Lydon's 'Marian' café'. And he was too big to argue with.

Mícheál had certainly done his best for us in Galway. Meeting us off the train that first night – our taxi was his father's lorry – he had driven us directly from Eyre Square to Barna to meet his father, and to show us where he came from. Well maybe not too directly because we went by way of the docks, and had already met Brendan O'Donnell. It was a rather sad house that we came into. Mícheál's mother had died suddenly only six or eight weeks previously, and his father, John Canning carried his grief in that way many Irishmen have; outwardly apologetic that things were not as they would have been if she were there. Inside, this was a tragedy on top of others. Two of their four sons had been lost, one by drowning, the other in a road accident. Mícheál himself, it was said, was refused to Death by a priest that came on him after a terrible accident near the Warwick Hotel in Salthill. "This cannot be allowed" he was heard to say "This family has lost too much already".

This was Galway; the starting point for Aran and Connemara and Cois Fhairrge; a place and a people with both a deep spirituality and a belief in the spirit world, where the supernatural was just another face on life. I am certain I wrote of it. A letter a week to Lilian Feeney, more or less; two, sometimes three, to Clare; once a fortnight to my mother; an occasional letter to Kevin Dillon. I even wrote my father, one of the few I ever wrote to him. What with postage, cinema, coffee and cakes, Ceile and Old-time once a week, an odd few bottles of stout, ten shillings never went so far.

It helped that we had Mícheál as a friend. After the first, uncomfortable night, when Dennis Daly and I shared a small single bed in Mícheál's home in Barna – remember, Dennis, if not three foot broad, seemed it – he introduced us to Jim Carroll, who was a partner in a small garage in the Claddagh, and to his wife, who agreed to take us as boarders. Mícheál had the imp of movement in him, and when agitated could strut better than Mussolini. His particular thing was to call for us in the evening, driving the father's car – a Standard 10 – and take us anywhere from the docks to Carraroe, or beyond. On the first night he took us to Leitir Mór, to see his girlfriend Berni O'Toole, he cut the engine and coasted past the house in Barna going back because, he said, his father would recognise the sound of the car. At Berni O'Tooles house he left us sitting outside in the car for the guts of an hour then shoe'd it on the way back to Galway, doing the thirty-one miles in thirty-one minutes – even with coasting again past the house in Barna. I can still feel Dennis Daly's big hands in the small of my back, so tightly did he grip the back of my seat. But this five foot seven, untypically blonde Connemara man showed us his special place; Barna and Furbo, Spiddal, Rossaveal and Sruthán; Casla and Carraroe; Cuan an Fhir Mhóir. Cois Fhairrge and its people.

"Are you going back West?" was more simply said in Irish: "An bhfuil tú ag dul siar?" the word siar standing for both 'back' and 'west'. It was perhaps the commonest phrase to be heard outside the railway station at Eyre Square, where the buses for Connemara awaited the passenger trains from Dublin. It was a question put to myself drawing on to one weekend out into 1959. There was to be a Gaelic Drama festival in Carna, and that was beyond our explorations up till then, involving a circuitous journey around Kilkerrin Bay. It was a Connemara girl named Cáit Ní Coisdealbha

169

who asked me. She was a sister of Johnny Choill Mhaidhc, who was then achieving a name for himself as a writer and a playwright, and had won 'Bonn Óir' an Oireachtais! Cait worked as a telephonist in the exchange in Galway, but I met her at the 'Réalt', a club run by a Praesidium of the Legion of Mary. At Carna, she was to appear in 'An Tinncéara Bui' - 'The Yellow Tinker' – the one act play by her brother Johnny, that had won the gold medal in Dublin. A young bank clerk, from either Laois or Offaly, whom I had also met at the 'Realt' offered me a lift out on the back of his motorbike. We got there uneventfully, travelling via Oughterard, Maam Cross and Screeb rather than by the coast road, and enjoyed a long afternoon and evening of drama. The winning director for a full-length play was a young English woman, Irene Gordon. Lancashire-born of a Latvian mother, who had recently been appointed Jubilee Nurse for the area, she hadn't a word of Irish. But her's is another story. It was Cáit Ní Coisdealbha's portrayal of the bargirl charmed from home by the playing of the 'Yellow Tinker' – by the tune and the man – that fascinated me. When, almost two years later I sat in that flat in Greystones where I had gone one winter's evening more for comfort than cuddles, and heard the girl on my knee say "Lets go away together, Jago; I have some money saved up" I knew that deep down she meant it. Knew that there was a desperate urge to escape in so many Irish people.

In that winter of 58-59 I think I felt I had escaped, or at least found the means to do so. In my letters I could write what I would have felt too awkward to say, while all the time mixing with people daily whose very existence was a river of talk. The scarcity of money, far from being a hindrance to social intercourse, became the very stimulus of it. The evenings we went back to Barna with Mícheál were especially good; when we went back the road to the Tailliur's – Míchaél ó Cíosóig, the tailor – who livened our conversations with his own interest in the worldly doings, and showed us how to build a turf fire in the hearth. That is when he was not sitting lotus-fashion on the sturdy linoleum-topped table, sewing. Sewing delicate even stitches, and at such speed, in heavy wool 'ceann-easna' or twill, that could do service as material for bullet-proof vests. On other evenings we just crossed the road to the old 'Cailleach's' house, with its lifetime's collection of mugs exciting our greed, even in the dusky light of the oil lamp. Yet another item that stirred my covetousness was an old blackened 'spilléad' – Billy, John and I would have called it a trough – suspended from even blacker rafters over the half-loft. It held the remnants of an ancient longline. Afterwards we would cross back over the road to 'Ma Donnelley's' for a pint or a bottle of stout, and to meet the Táillíur, and to go in fear of losing our drink. If we hadn't all drunk up in time – and the conversation could turn that lively that we might not have – all unfinished glasses were poured down the sink at five minutes to closing time.

Don't ask me where I got the fare to go to London, to Bushey, for Christmas; but I did. And went on to Birmingham to Claire for two or three days of romance and nights of barely celibate passion, and detoured to Greystones on my way back to Galway. I had arranged to take Rita Dunn to the Gaelic Pantomime in the Abbey Theatre, but thought to call on some people beforehand. Now I remember for certain that I had a glass of whiskey and ham sandwiches in Kinsellas house in Blacklion – it was the last time I visited Jim and Kitty, and Jim's wife, for I think he was married by then – and walked on to Killincarrig to my Aunt May's. After that you could take your pick of Duffy's, Smullen's, Twamley's or Dillon's, but I have a vague remembrance of saying cheerio to Uncle Bernie in the Wicklow Arms and getting the bus from Delgany to Bobby Mooney's shop in Greystones. The 'John McKenzie' name and the beautiful signal red front had already gone. By the time I climbed into an 'apple-pie' bed, spiked with holly, in the Summerhill Hotel that night, and fell asleep to the giggles of Rita and Kathleen Dunn who had delayed below in the hall, I had some day. And by the time I got back to Galway the following evening and snored so loudly all through the night that I kept two houses awake, I had some holiday.

The money to travel to Kathleen and Eric's wedding, some time in February, is more easily explained. I had been fighting to get workman's compensation over the head of a poisoned finger I developed when the 'Loch Lorgan' was fishing the new nylon 'Vinge trawl' for herring off Dunmore East. It was that bad at the time I had to sign-off and hitched my way home. The Bord was resisting my claim, but Dr MacCartan had written "it was a stab-wound that penetrated almost to the Peri-ostium" and I was sure this would swing it. Paying full 'stamp' meant we were covered for workmen's compensation, and I was determined to get value for my two shillings and thruppences. The week it finally came through, I got an invitation to Kathleen and Eric's wedding on the Tuesday; on Wednesday a telegram to say it was off; on Thursday the cheque – thirteen pounds ten shillings representing three weeks at four pounds ten – and on Friday a telegram to say it was on, and that I was to give her away. That's how I came to be standing in John and Jean's flat off Wood Green in London in my underpants the next morning.

Desperate to get married and go off to Canada with Eric, and knowing Mother and Father could not afford the cost in the circumstances of the time, Kay and Eric had sent out the invitations themselves. And for Mother and Father at the time that just wasn't on. Especially as the invitations were worded "Mr and Mrs J. Hayden invite---". Its drawing on to their fortieth wedding anniversary, Kathleen and Eric's that is, and they're still together; and they still have the Waterford Crystal liqueur glasses that my workman's compensation paid for along with the trip to London.

By the time I sat the exam for the skipper's ticket I was seriously short of cash, and was running out of money even for postage stamps. I was still writing as often as ever to both Claire and Lilian Feeney, the friendships deepening all the time, each in its own special way. Moriarty of the Bord got me away to sea on the 'Loch Lein' with the old German skipper, Rheinin Sittik, and we sailed for the Minch. It was my first trip north to the Hebrides, and my first and only trip with the sixty-five-year-old skipper. I never forgot either. The beaches on the islands, dazzlingly white in the mid April sun, contrasted with rocky isolated crags port and starboard. The lighthouses of Ruadh Re, Dhu Artic and Skerryvore came and went; Skerryvore merely a needle on the horizon as we approached it, and no more than a needle as we breasted it and let it fall away astern.

It was a simple fall that did for me, maybe eight days into the trip, and after twenty-four hours of agony, sufficed for everyone else on board. We had endured nothing but hardship from the first moment we shot the trawl away in the North Minch. Bad ground, bags of small haddock that had all to be gutted, no cod, hake or jumbo haddies, nets torn every time. We 'paralysed' six times in forty-eight hours, and I know I put in one continuous spell of fiftytwo and a half hours on deck. The skipper himself spent three whole days on his own in the wheelhouse, seeming to exist only on porridge with a slab of butter and a raw egg in it, and hot thick tea. He ran out of cigarettes. The cook said he ran out of vegetables. But I was the excuse that finally took us all into Stornaway; all over a knock on my knee from a stumble over a pound board as I tried to clear a float when we were shooting away.

I never fully understood the phrase 'paralytic' before, never in my life saw men as drunk; but the story of how horizontal they were, falling out of the 'Crit' bar, and of what happened when we were directed into Fleetwood for the worst market in five years, will keep. Back in Dublin I was paid off with eight pounds and ninepence – we had another pound of a sub to go to Blackpool – and I limped onto the mailboat, and didn't check till I turned in the door of the studio flat in Bushey. Back to base, bruised in body and spirit; financially paralysed.

I got a job in Ellam's duplicator factory off Water Lane, down at the bottom of the Avenue, and limped my way in, in the mornings, and home again in the evenings, and stood on one leg like a stork all day.

I continued writing my letters. On the Birmingham front things became even better. After three weeks I ventured up for a weekend, catching the electric line train from Watford Junction to Euston and connecting with the express to Birmingham. After that first weekend, I hitched, taking the bus first to St. Albans, then walking out the A5 to a traffic lights just on the edge of town. I found I could beat the train, though I always took the train back on Sunday evenings, for certainty. For me it was an exploration; for her and I together a succession of romantic excursions in an England I didn't know existed. Malvern, where Queen Boadicea defied the Romans. Stratford-on-Avon. The Cotswolds, totally rural, peppered with pale yellow stone villages and occasional isolated pubs. Windsor, the castle I never saw because we dallied in the park.

Summer drew on. Lilian Feeney's letters touched on her pending visit to London. Before I met her the previous year she met and fell for a young Englishman who worked for the BBC. He visited her parents at Easter, and she was to meet his in summer. I wrote other letters, job hunting. An Irish fisheries research vessel was planned, and I was interested in getting a job on it. I wrote to different places; the American Embassy; to Russia; hoping to get research vessel experience. The Ministry of Agriculture Fisheries and Food in Lowestoft passed my letter on to St. Andrew's House in Edinburgh, and they sent me a telegram with instructions to join the 'FRS Scotia' in Leith. I think the date stipulated was the fourth of July. At the time I hadn't received a letter from Lilian for just over a fortnight, and while it puzzled me, I placed no particular significance on it. But I think among the first things I did in Edinburgh were to send her and Claire J. Arthur Dixon postcards.

Over the next seven months we anchored at more than forty different places off the coast of Scotland and it's islands, from Castle Bay in Barra to Saxa in Shetland to Cruden Bay, and while I was ashore only in Oban, Stornaway, Lerwick, Balta, Inverness and Invergordon, apart from Leith and Aberdeen, it seemed all those

174

places had been captured by J. Arthur Dixon on his postcards. Captured in all their moods also. But that first postcard to Lilian Feney was nearly the last. A letter from her finally caught up with me. There is a moment in the Stephen Spielberg film, Jaws 2, where a youngster, discovered hiding in the forward cuddy of a bitten-in-two sailing dinghy, tries desperately to tell what had happened, and with chest heaving stutters for what seems like minutes. "The Sh--- the sh- sh--- the sh sh sh". Then the dam bursts. "The Shaaaaark". Lilian's letter was like that final moment. Engaged, and to have it broken off, all in a week. It took six weeks for the shriek to rip through the pain, and the only one she could direct it to was me. What instant shoulders I had to grow.

Three voyages I made on the 'Scotia'; A water-sampling trip over and back to the coast of Norway, working a grid pattern, never seeing Norway because we neared it always at night; to the Minch and the Western Isles; and to 'Shetland'. There I signed off – I was a relief man – and travelled back to Leith to do relief on the fishery cruiser 'Longa', a protection vessel. The Saturday night boat from Lerwick, the 'St. Clair', made heavy weather of a south-easterly gale, and we docked three hours late in Aberdeen. The train I then connected with left me late into Edinburgh. I made my way to Leith docks knowing that the watchman aboard would already be in his bunk, with only a tilly-lamp for light. That's how I found him, Willie McKay. "Cibé mar a thán tu?" he greeted me and I replied "Táim go maith, gura maith agat, agus cé chaoi bhfuil tu féin". "Aha" he said, " I thought you looked as if you might know the Gallic". He was married and living in the village of Cromarty, but had been born in Ballintore where my father used throw the wartime powdered egg to the gulls – at a time when the 'Gallic' was still spoken locally. In my time on the 'Scotia' I managed one visit to Birmingham, travelling on an overnight train, and I remember sticking my head out the window into a moonlit night as we sped off Shap Summit in Cumberland. This was exactly where the world speed record for a steam-locomotive was made. It was a glorious night replete with that marvellous feeling one gets on a fast night train; ones journey entrusted to others in the assurance of being delivered safely in the morning; and it was a steam-train. I made one other journey south only, down to Bushey, and hitched back – well almost; I nearly made it to Newcastle-on-Tyne – but I kept writing, and kept sending J. Arthur Dixon postcards.

The 'Longa' was stationed in the Moray Firth and patrolled the coast from Cape Wrath to Berwick-on-Tweed. For the most part we ventured no further north than the Pentland Firth, and came south of Fraserburgh only as far as Cruden Bay. When we lay to anchor, it was usually just outside or just inside the Cromarty Firth, though at weekends we came in through the 'Sutors' – the headlands marking the mouth of the firth to tie up at Invergordon. The mail, however, was directed to Cromarty village, and was collected by one of the leading seamen who went ashore in the Z-boat. Outgoing mail went ashore with him, to be posted in Cromarty. On this one particular occasion I had a 'jumbo' Arthur Dixon postcard already written and stamped, and addressed to Claire in Birmingham. I couldn't tell you now what was on either the front or the back of it, though it was special to me then. The mail collected that day, and brought out to the ship by leading seaman Jimmy Gillies, included one letter to me. From Birmingham. From Claire. She had met someone else. His name was Mike. He was nice, like me, but she felt it would be different. He would not have been a Roman Catholic as I was. She was Church of England, but favoured Methodism or Methodists. This difference had been a problem for us, for her and for me. It would be better this way. But it wasn't. Mike was RC also.

Chapter Twenty Four – The Beginning of Fear?

The 'Wizard of Oz' is a great favourite of mine, and I have both seen the movie and have read the original story by Frank L. Baum. I especially like the character of the 'Cowardly Lion'. When my wife and I had children of our own, I bought a long-playing record of the story – it cost tenshillings and sixpence – and I'm sure it has been played a thousand times. When the character giving voice to the lion, after he has killed the 'Crocobear', protests his cowardice in a New York accent – "I was just terribly afraid somebody might get hoit" it's just something else. My own courage is more or less at one with this; but it wasn't always so.

I haven't a memory earlier than two and a half, but I know that as an infant I developed a serious abscess on my right leg, high up in the groin, and this was lanced by Dr. Mitchell, using as I understand it a red hot needle. I carry the entry and exit marks of it yet. This is certainly what led Aunt Lizzie, my mother's Godmother, and Sisters Rupert and Josephine of the Holy Faith who were sisters of Fan Donohoe, Father's Godmother, to speak of me always as 'poor wee Jimmy'. Nobody could be wee-er, or nicer, than Rupert and Josephine; they were tiny people, but this declamation of theirs was something that always got to me. I sometimes wonder if it was the thing that triggered my temper in the first place; not when they said it, but when others might have. Blood up, I would have advanced un-armed on live cannon.

When I was growing up there was a paling around the cove in front of the Grand Hotel. It started where the small, low wall in front of Carrig Eden Hotel ended, and stretched as far as the grassy patch at the back of the rocks. It was made of split branches; bound together top and bottom by twisted bull-wire. We were easily able to slip inside the fence where the low wall ended – we used walk along the top of this even though there was an eight or ten foot drop on the sea side of it – and would then make our way along the wee track that skirted the edge of the cove. We usually squeezed back out onto the road at one or two places where a paling batten was broken, but occasionally we braved it right to the end, picking our steps carefully past the big drop which must have been twenty or twenty five feet. It was clearly dangerous, and the County Council replaced it with a six-inch concrete wall; and plastered it and rounded the top after the fashion of the time. I've not just walked that; I've run it; end to end along the top of the wall; and was no older than seven or eight.

I was older, maybe nine, when I decided I knew the road so well from my Grandfather's shop to the cottage in the 'Bawn' that I could ride my bicycle the full length of it with my eyes shut. It was summertime, and every morning I did one or two of the paper rounds for my grandfather. After I had finished one morning, I decided to test myself. I determined to get on the bicycle and ride the full length of Trafalgar Rd., down the hill at St.Killians Hall, swing round the bend at the white house that was named 'Upton', and then all the way over the road past Dann's and Duncairn Terrace to Pennycook's.

I gave myself two advantages; I waited until the bus from Bray that came through about half past nine or twenty to ten had gone; and I crossed over to the other side of the road from the shop before sitting into the saddle at the kerb. One last peek, then I closed my eyes, not too tightly – I mean I didn't screw them up – and pushed myself off. I took it steadily, not too slow, not my usual frantic pedalling either. Past the Presbyterian Church. Past Lewis's hotel. Past Mrs Fanning's. If you were to ask me now, I'd say that I was navigating by sound, what with the purr of the tyres on the road, and the changing character of the echoes from the different houses in the street. That from Lewis's being different from the wall of Mrs Fanning's garden, and it in turn from the slab of her house. Beyond that, the gap where Marine Terrace stretched past the barracks, let in the sound of the sea. Then followed the bit past the back of the Grand Hotel. At this point I got a bit curious and I peeked. Just once. I was almost level with Aunt Lizzie's house, and had already covered about two hundred yards. My line was true, about five feet out from the kerb; nothing was coming, so I shut my eyes again and pedalled on. The gradual incline to the top of the hill took effect now, and as I passed the opening of Sidmonton road where the fall really started, level with the Miss Porters' little drapery shop, I let the bike freewheel as it accelerated of its own accord. One final rush; past Cool-na-Greine and the YWCA; past the hall; past Gething's; then as the bike slowed at Upton's, I started to pedal furiously and swung round the bend.

"What If Paddy Daly and the horse comes out of Johnston Mooney and O'Brien's with the bread-van?" I thought, and a bit of panic set in. I tried to keep pedalling, but the doubt wouldn't let go so I finally opened my eyes. I was almost level with the door of the bar. I had made it to Jackie Dann's. I never again attempted it, even though I was right on line at the end, nor ever attempted anything remotely like it. True I jumped over and back from the 'Ard Aidhm' to the 'Pride of Ulster', to take a photograph, while we were steaming in the Irish Sea; and I walked the rail of the 'Scotia' as we breasted the distant early warning radar scanner at Buchan Ness just south of Peterhead in Scotland one afternoon. But I lost something that morning in Greystones. Even though I succeeded, I realised I had gone too far. Maybe it's fanciful to think that now, but I was born into a world that had gone too far, and would go further still. At that age I knew no such profundities, but I think it was the point from which I attempted to edge in my temper. I think also, for me, it was the beginning of fear.

The noise that terrified me as a child, that harshly explosive combination of compressor and rock drill as the army engineers bored chargeholes into the stone of the railway arch, I still edge away from, not from fear, but because it is painful. But you would scarcely register the decibels of a compressor these days; so much has noise become a constant of our environment. It's as if the world has become afraid of that silence in which a child might hear the ripple of waves against the planks of a rowing boat from that hunkered-down position in the bow into which only a child can fit. One of those 'safe' places. Another place that we usually associate with being 'safe' is the bedroom, yet it was in the small bedroom in 'Novara', our house in Blacklion, that I had one of the most terrifying experiences of my life. It was a winter night. Dark. At a guess, the year was 1943 or 1944. Our mother was away down to my grandfather's shop in the town on the big ladies bicycle. I think she was writing up the books for him. I had been put to bed, and either Billy or John left in charge. I think I must have had a nightmare, about eternity, and woke screaming. I didn't want to live "for ever and ever". What triggered it I don't remember. I suppose the existence of a God with whom we would live without end – if we were good – had been drilled into us at school by either the nun or the brother; and also its corollary; that if bad, we would burn without end. Whatever it was, I sobbed my heart out that night, and was distressed by it for months.

The first film I ever saw also upset me. It was a drama set in logging country, and depicted great trees being cut down and roads being bulldozed through the forest. It ran as a feature along with a stage show in the Theatre Royal, and it was the matinee stage show my Mother wanted to see that afternoon that she brought me. She didn't fancy the film either, nor liked the terrifying forest-fire scenes that bothered me. Mother wasn't a great one for films at any time, and I think one of the reasons may have been that the first film Father brought her to was 'Dracula'. Or so she once said. I'm sure it was in Hipple's picture house, with its one projector and pauses in total darkness while reels were changed. The lights were turned on at reel changes only if the audience got too rowdy. Not my mother's scene at all.

It was in Hipple's that I had my first encounter with Bela Lugosi's 'Dracula'. The film was 'House of Dracula', and it featured also Lon

Chaney as the 'Wolf Man', and Boris Karloff in the role of a doctor. Dessie Murphy said afterwards that it had more monsters in it than any of those other films, what with the Boris Karloff character being mad, and the hunchback nurse. He counted also the mad doctor of Half-Moon Street and the mad doctor of Full-Moon Street although I don't remember seeing them. The piece-de-resistance of course was the Frankenstein monster itself, whose body was discovered in a sea-cave into which Lon Chaney had been washed by the storm after he jumped over the cliff. On the night of the full moon of course. Its no wonder I didn't remember the mad doctors of Half or Full-Moon Streets; it's a wonder I remember anything of the film at all. I was down behind the back of the seat, with my eyes closed. I had been tagging along after the 'big' fellows as usual, like Dessie, who were able to take it, and had convinced my mother that I was big enough to go; and as usual she relented. Dessie's other comment at the time was that it wasn't as scary as 'Frankenstein Meets the Wolf-Man', but I don't know. Its theme of the transference of terrifying afflictions by blood transfusions has become all too real, what with Aids, Hepatitis C and new-variant CJD. Back then, my terror as always lay in my imagination. It was summer, and we were in Mrs Archer's cottage in the 'Bawn', but that year I had been billeted out to Tom Keddy's front-room in number four. Getting to bed was the problem. I had to leave the safety of number two, with the kitchen light on, and the radio playing, and the two bits of curtain drawn; and make a racing drive for Tom Keddy's, in through the front and bedroom doors with their awkward old-fashioned latches, and into the bed and under the blankets, trousers shoes and socks still on. And latch the doors behind me of course. I was certain the monster lurked in Tom Keddy's shed where the heavily catecued herring nets hung un-used for years across oars that could only have belonged to that lumpy old skiff of his that didn't see the water in my time.

Through time I eventually came to terms with these creatures of the imagination, and read Bram Stoker's classic, 'Dracula', as well as 'The Lair of the White Worm'. I even attempted 'The Mysteries of

Udolpho' in an old copy I requested in the reading room of the National Library in Kildare Street. It was heavy going, what with it's 'Caftles' for castles, but it had the reputation of being the fore-runner of all these gothic mystery tales, and was written by yet another Dublin author, a Mrs Ann Radcliffe. Bram Stoker's novel is perhaps the more enduring, certainly for us of that particular film-going generation that still cherish Bela Lugosi's delivery of "The children of the night. What sweet music they make". And when, in recent years, mad about a Saturday morning given to golf, I walked the two and a half miles to town, and took McGeehan's coach a further one hundred and sixty five miles to Dublin to enjoy Martin Landau's Oscar-winning performance in 'Ed Wood', then showing at the 'Light House' cinema, I had no remorse. The total absence of remorse was the key characteristic in Mary Shelley's monster, and Boris Karloff captured it totally in James Whale's film of the book, despite the laughable scene in which 'Igor', having smashed the glass jar with the desired brain, lifts another to the camera clearly displaying it's label "criminal type brain". The director should never have doubted the power of Boris Karloff's cold unblinking eyes. They conveyed everything Mary Shelley wrote into the character. The funny thing is, Karloff gave the creature a certain humanity, and this she did not intend. But it is the real reason we remember the film so well. What might Shakespeare's Scottish play become were it to be filmed as a monster movie; Macbeth the man – his own words say it – twisted into a monster by the deviousness of what few women touch his life. Betrayed at the end by a man un-born of woman, he finally attempts to become man again in that great declamation "Lead on MacDuff and damned be him that first cries, "Hold, enough". Were I such a film's promoter, I would arrange for the audience at the movie's premier to be sprayed with spurts of real blood at the climax.

The true monsters were the Hitler's and the Stalin's, the Beria's and the Eichman's. They were aped by the Ceasescus' and have their latter-day counterparts in Serbia's Milosevic and Bosnia's Karadjzic.

We have been relatively lucky in Ireland because, aside from the death-masters of the IRA, we have had only grubby little thieves. These men and their like were monsters because they emptied themselves of humanity, set it aside totally. In our Judaeo-Christian tradition it is only because we are human that we can be redeemed. Peter could not have been saved had he not first sunk. But one wonders if this God that sent part of him/her self, the Christ, to become human so that we might be saved needed our humanity to save itself. Now there's a tremulous thought. But we lived through real terror, even if we managed to distance ourselves from it to live. I made a character in a short-story I wrote even before Yuri Gagarin became the first man in space, think: "Someday, somebody, somewhere, will just press a button, and the entire earth will dissolve". The Americans had already dissolved a significant piece of it, a cubic mile, in their first H-bomb explosion at Eniwetok in the Marshall Islands. Britain stood men up in the Australian desert, as cynically as it had sent them for King and Country across the barbed wire in the First World War's madness, to see how they would fare. The Soviet Union spied on everyone and killed or exiled a family member in one in every four of its own people's families. And the Americans instructed their children in school what to do in the event of an Atomic attack. Don't tell me this wasn't an age of terror.

When I sailed from Aberdeen on my first trip on the 'Scotia', having overnighted there to pick up Marine Laboratory scientists after a short voyage from Leith, we were only a couple of hours clear of the port, when we passed abreast of a great radar scanner on the headland of Buchan Ness, just south of Peterhead. The head is one of those notable geographical points of Britain, such as Land's End or Cape Wrath or the Mull of Kintyre. The radar scanner had counterparts elsewhere, at Fylingdale in Yorkshire and at Saxa in Shetland. They were parts of the DEW line – Distant Early Warning. Distant from America, that is, so that if Russia were to launch missiles against the West, the Americans might get some warning as Western Europe was annihilated. And for that reason the scanners rotated constantly, day and night. They never stopped. So all the seamen on the research vessel told me. Not in their time at sea. But a morning came when they did stop, and I was there to see it.

Our trip had taken us to Shetland where we were trying a German net with heavy bobbin ground-gear, and hauled it by the bang-up method. That is, we tightened the entire length of the ground-rope between the for'ard and after gallows, and either pushed or pulled as it was slacked off, depending on whether we were shooting or hauling. We fished just to the east of Balta, which is on the northernmost island, and came to anchor every evening in the Balta Sound, just inside a small island. In the mornings as we steamed off from the shore and opened up the land, the constant motion of the Saxa radar scanner could clearly be seen. It topped a headland just to the north of Balta. I was detailed as anchor-watch that trip, and usually turned-in just after eight in the morning, rising again for the mid-day meal about twelve. Coming on deck one particular morning, I immediately saw through the foc'sle door that the giant scanner was stopped. I asked Johnny Annand, the bos'un, and some of the other seamen if they had actually seen it stop. Nobody had. In the afternoon it came to me; that was the day Kruschev landed in the USA on his visit to the United Nations.

Our work in the area finished, we left the grounds for home, over-nighting only in Lerwick to take on water and stores. In the afternoon of the day after leaving Lerwick, as we approached Peterhead, I scanned ahead myself to see if Buchan Ness scanner was operating. It was still. I watched it tightly, never taking my eyes off it for a second as we drew abeam, first of Peterhead, then of the Ness itself, and continued as it fell away behind us. Suddenly, it started. It was the day, and almost the hour that Kruschev departed the United States.

It was four or five months later that I left Scotland for Dublin to take up a berth on the first Irish fisheries research vessel, the Cú Feasa, that was nearing completion in Holland. Scotland was snow-bound.

Five children of seventeen that were left off a tractor in Aberdeenshire in an attempt to get them home from school, never made it the rest of the way and were lost in the white-out. The newspapers carried reports of the RAF Mountain Rescue Team. Commander Macrae of the 'Longa' responded to a telegram from St. Andrew's House in Edinburgh instructing him to put me ashore by steaming to Aberdeen, where I could take a train to Glasgow. Only one other person shared the compartment with me as we pulled out of Aberdeen, and he was wearing a blue RAF greatcoat and was carrying a pair of what I took to be climbing boots. After a while I got talking to him, and asked if he was a member of the mountain rescue team. "No" he said. He was a Yorkshire man and was into pot holing. He was homeward bound from Shetland on furlough, and hoped to do a bit of caving. I asked him if he was stationed at Saxa, and narrated my observations of it and Buchan Ness. I suppose the time was used for over-haul, I speculated. But I got nothing out of him. He clammed up totally; even moved to the far corner of the compartment. An Irishman to ask such questions! I endured two and a half hours of silence into Glasgow, and I suppose it was lucky there was no intervening stop. I might have been 'lifted' from the train.

Chapter Twenty Five – Hair All Curling Gold

I wrote of a character in yet another of my short stories that he "drew his loneliness about him like a comfort-blanket", and Tony O'Callaghan thought it a terrible image. But that's what its like. I've been there. I sometimes think that God Himself – or Herself, if that is your interpretation – has been there also. "In the beginning was the Word" John tells us "and the Word was with God". It was later that he created the Firmament and divided Heaven from Earth; not too different from the Chaos of the Greeks, out of which the Cosmos was created; nor yet from the evolution of chemistry in space as so brilliantly re-discovered by today's astronomers and astrophysicists. But that was not enough; there was no company in it, and so He created Man. "Male and Female he created them. And God saw that it was good".

I don't know if God can be lonely, but in my life, from 1957 on there was an increasing edge of loneliness. My friends were marvellous, and my relations were always there, and my adventures throughout those years added ever-new dimensions to my life. But when I walked the roads at night, usually but not always secure that I had a bed for the night, I was conscious that it was not my own. There were nights that were brilliantly full of shooting stars, and others in which I paused when taking a shortcut across Greystones Golf Club perhaps either from Mrs Duffys or to Aunt Mays, to wonder at the Northern Lights which played white, red and green symphonies in the northern sky. The black bulk of Bray Head screened off the lights of Dublin City which then were minor by comparison with the massive orange glow that now occurs. And there were other, cold, damp nights when I just felt particularly alone.

The worst - the loneliest that is – occurred a couple of years on. I was staying for a couple of days with my brother Billy, who by then was working for the Irish Sugar Company, and with his wife Margaret at their house in Mallow; and set off to hitchhike to

Killarney for the day. I had been in Killarney once previously, with Jimmy Smullen and his girlfriend Peggy, together with Sean Dillon, on a Radio Train excursion – the time the motor went on fire – and had enjoyed it. This was to be a second visit. Setting off that morning I took ill out along the Navigation road, and almost turned back. After an hour and a half sitting at the side of the road, during which time I puked several times, I decided to press on and eventually made it to Killarney, but late. I was late leaving therefore, though it was still daylight, and the lifts were poor, a mile here, three, maybe five there. I walked on, thinking to find one of those 'good' spots where almost any motorist would stop. There were none. As it darkened it came on to drizzle; a solid, down-falling, West Cork drizzle. It's a funny thing about drizzle at night; nothing else is quite so dark. Even I, who was used to walking at night, had difficulty keeping on the road. I was wearing a respectable enough tweed suit, but had only sandals and socks on my feet. After a couple of hours I was halfway between Killarney and Mallow, and could feel the water running down my skin everywhere. Spotting a light I trudged towards it, and found myself looking in an uncurtained window at a woman and four teen-aged girls. I wanted to knock at the door; to ask if I could perhaps sleep in their shed for the night; but I held back. How the hell could I knock at any door in the state I was in? Bearded. A stranger. Water running out of me. I walked on into the night. Later, some Samaritan lifted me and left me at the bottom of my road in Mallow. His car seat must have been wet for days.

Co-incidence played a big part in my life in those days; and what the earlier near incantations of grand-aunts Lizzie, Rupert and Josephine of "Wee Jimmy" or "poor wee Jimmy", and the regularity of my stays in hospital – in 1950, and again in 1953 and 1956, and with the knock on the knee in 1959 - I almost started to think I was like one of those faulty cars that is all the time being taken back to the repair shop. The co-incidences were real. When I attempted door-to-door vacuum cleaner selling and worked with Pat Quinn, he told me of a man named Phil McCreesh who had been a successful smuggler, and who once owned three lorries. But times had gone against him and he had gone to England. And when I despaired of the vacuum cleaner selling and went to England myself, within a matter of six weeks I had met that same Phil McCreesh. He was a British Railway porter. Then he got promotion and became a guard on the Glasgow night train.

The co-incidences didn't stop there, nor with the winning horses 'Beech Walk' and 'Must Fly' of Rita Dunn and the Enniskerry connection. When Sean Moriarity of the Irish Sea Fisheries Board, called up the operator to send a telegram to me to report to Dublin from Scotland, it was Rita's mother who took the line. They were both Kerry people and quick, and their passing the time of day extended to remarking on their mutual acquaintance with me. When I finally received the original telegram from St. Andrew's where it had been opened in case there was an emergency, I had already got the exact text twice over, once from Moriarty, and once from Mrs Dunn. Co-incidences such as these were on the one hand comforting, involving as they did a reconnection with the familiar, yet on the other they left a sense that something or someone else had more than a hand in our destiny. I wasn't exactly comfortable with that.

I wasn't comfortable with the way we were dealt with on the 'Cu Feasa' either, for all of the fact that I had come to like Sean Moriarty who as Operations Manager of the Board had the responsibility of looking after day to day matters of vessel and crew. But she remained the Department's ship. When we finally collected her and sailed her back from Holland it was made clear to us that no expense had been spared in acquiring her, but it had been all voted in the previous financial year; and in the current year the purse strings were to be tied off. Moriarty had telegramed me earlier in Scotland, when the 'Longa' was into Inverness with a cracked boiler, to get me to phone him, which I did. I probably wouldn't be considered for the job of skipper, he said, or mate. Would I take a job on the deck? I said I would. I also added that I had my passport, could find my way around, and could go direct to Holland from Scotland. "What pay are you on", he asked, and I said: "Such and such pounds, plus one shilling and sixpence a day victualling allowance and grub yourself" "It will probably be the same" he said to the pay "and probably the same victualling allowance and conditions also".

John Glansford from Dunlaoghaire and Nicky McLaughlin from Howth who were the other two fellows taken on for the deck, had been told "There will probably be a 'chafing gear' allowance" – for seaboots and oilskins – and probably be a share of the catch". There were neither. The pay was a pound a week less than I got in Scotland, the victualling allowance a mere shilling a day, and I wasn't allowed my expenses from Scotland to Dublin, although that was where I was instructed to report. Had I travelled from Scotland to Holland to join the ship I would have been entitled to expenses in accordance with normal Merchant Navy conditions. It was a bad start. It wasn't as bad a start as that of the vessel itself. It failed to meet Dutch Board of Trade requirements and was not passed as seaworthy. On the day after we travelled overnight from Dunlaoghaire, while I was taking John Glansford to Hammersmith to visit his sister, accompanied by Nicky McLaughlin; and Sean Moriarity along with Tom Donohoe the cook were killing the day in London before meeting up at Kings Cross in the evening for the Harwich boat train; the Cú Feasa was taken out on a trial and had listed badly. When the three of us eventually got to Kings Cross, Moriarty was waiting frantically with instructions to get us back to Dublin. We eventually made it to Holland ten days later, after the vessel had been extensively altered. Chunks were chopped out of the masts. The original rails were cut off and replaced with lighter ones. I think the main winch may have been changed. I acquired a copy of the original profile drawing and I have it to this day, because it showed one other thing: The average of the overall length and the length between perpendiculars fell just under seventy five feet. This vessel had been designed to work commercially within the new baselines introduced by Erskine Childers in 1959. It was true to that mistaken policy of imposing artificial length restrictions that has plagued our fishing industry ever since, and continues in the form of EU ceilings on tonnage and horsepower.

We should join the union, we all said, but the question was which union? The Seamen's Union, it was decided, and it was left to me to search out the 'Seamen's Union of Ireland'. I eventually found their offices on the upper floor of a two-storey building near the Strand Cinema, with the foot of the stairs, which was at the back of a narrow hallway, guarded by two young women with their bottomsides tightly wrapped in half-a-yard skirts. I don't know if they were put there on purpose but they deflected both eye and intention. I penetrated the upper offices several times and met Charlie Fox, the General Secretary and Jimmy Hutton the treasurer. Once or twice only did I encounter Willie Stacey, the Assistant General Secretary, and both of those occasions were on the quayside. Charlie Fox, an old union hand with his roots in the British Seamen's Union, was able to explain to me the Trinity House origins of the victualling allowance, but the union did nothing for us. One day in Charlie Fox's office I read a telegram – upside down; I was good at that – from the crew of the 'Irish Cedar'. "Manchester" it read "is not too far from Dublin. We respectfully ask you to make the trip". Some hope. We couldn't get them to Sir John Rogersons Quay.

The year niggled on. Aleck Skoyles the skipper, a careful Scot, who had first come to Dublin in the late nineteen twenties with one of the vessels of the Dublin Steam Trawling Co, was regarded by crew who sailed with him as an owner's man. On the Cú Feasa he attempted to combine the needs of scientific fishing – hauls of no more than one hour duration – with the demands of commercial fishing as he understood it – fishing around the clock. Flesh and blood couldn't stick it, and with nothing extra in it for us, we bargained out a more sensible arrangement. I made one mistake though. Early enough on,

I wrote a letter to the editor of the 'Irish times' who replied: " Your article appears to indicate appalling mismanagement by the Bord in its relationships with its employees----" I still have his letter; and mine.

Ashore, I took to ceile-going; Sunday nights in the Mansion House; occasionally Saturday nights in Barry's Hotel. Lewy O'Rourke and I went to the 'Fleadh Cheoil' in Boyle, travelling from Dublin on an excursion special from Westland Row. One of two young women seated across the table from us and with whom we had got into conversation suddenly asked me "An tú Séamus Ó h-Aodáin". Co-incidence again. She was a sister of Cáit Ni Coisdealbha, and had never met or seen me before; merely heard of me. The 'Fleadh' was marvellous and Lewy and I shared a two man 'bivouac' tent that we pitched high up a field overlooking both town and railway station. When we had exhausted each day of music and enjoyment, we turned in at about four in the morning to the sound of ceile tunes somewhere out the Roscommon Road; and when we woke to the sun at half-past seven or eight in the morning, it appeared the same tunes were still being played.

Liam McCoy and Michael McGillicuddy from Enniskerry were at the Fleadh, along with another fellow who spent most of the day drawing thumbnail pencil sketches in a note pad of the musicians and characters. The girl friend of one of the men made up the foursome and they lived and slept the three nights in an old Ford Prefect car. McGillicuddy, a forester, was a Kerryman, but the others were either from Co. Wicklow or South County Dublin. They were all stalwarts from the ceiles in Enniskerry that Lewy O'Rourke organised. Liam McCoy had a lovely tenor voice, and when called on at the ceiles usually gave us a plaintive if sometimes too highly pitched rendering of 'The Lark in the Clear Air'. It was Liam I imitated that weekend home on the cheap British Rail ticket when I was railway portering, and had borrowed Lewy O'Rourkes bicycle for the last leg of the journey from Bray to Greystones. Freewheeling down Windgates, with a small bit of a shower standing out to sea at the back of the rocks, on my way to a lunch date – and late – with Maire Niellan and Lilian McGowan, I cracked the air with my imitation of Liam McCoy "And I hear the sweet La-ark sing i-in the cle-ear air of the day". Come to think of it, I must have met those two teachers first in 1957.

As the Fleadh wound up on Monday evening Lewy and I caught the last of the special excursion trains back to the city after the grand final Ceile in St. Joseph's Hall. We bunked down aboard the Cu Feasa and Lewy headed for home on the Tuesday morning while we put out to sea. It was the weekend before I met up with him again. Liam McCoy made it home in a fractured kind of a state either late on Tuesday or on the Wednesday and ventured cautiously into work on the Thursday. He was just finishing his tea in the evening, and wondering if he might chance a pint, when the phone rang. It was McGillicuddy.
"What would you like to hear, boy!"

"Eh?"

"What would you like to hear, Liam?"

He had a fiddler there. Still in Boyle. There was only the one answer:
"Play the "Batterin' Ram". It was the hot tune in Boyle that year. There was scarcely a phone call got out of Roscommon and half Mayo for the next three-quarters of an hour as all the manual exchanges linked into this last glorious session.

My own moment of glory, the following year was both equally brief, and in its way equally final. Francis Dowds assailed me coming from eight o'clock mass.
"Congratulations Jemmy, I see you've a win up on the crossword".

I had been watching the 'Sunday Review' crossword for six months, convinced a complete permutation could be done within the week. That particular crossword had been brought into the paper from the earlier 'Radio Review' which was the first newspaper to say "you may submit as many entries as you wish". All the other newspapers limited the number of entries. In addition, the 'Review' defined the words that were acceptable as alternatives in the answers to the clues.

The other papers hedged their bets, declaring that the winning solution would be that deemed most appropriate by a panel of judges, and presumably picked their winners with judicious regard to area and circulation. The crosswords were lucrative circulation boosters.

The 'Sunday Review' usually offered a splittable prize of £500, with a bonus of an extra £250 for a single outright winner. I knew myself that they had to be equally in control of the final selection of a winner, but when they offered a great double-week competition with a splittable prize of £750 and a bonus of £4250 for a single outright winner, I could resist no longer. To cap it all, the usual pattern of acceptable choices was fortuitously changed, and the total permutation dropped to – I think – six thousand one hundred and eighty four, from something about double that. And the Cu Feasa was in dry-dock, and we had been told to take leave.

I bought three hundred and thirty Sunday Reviews. Honest, I did. At the back-issues desk in the Irish Times office in Westmoreland Street. I went then and watched a double bill matinee in the Astor Cinema – one of them was Alain Resnais's 'Hiroshima Mon Amour' – and I travelled out to Greystones from Tara St. station wondering if I was mad. A bit of a table in the small bedroom in Jimmy and Peggy Smullen's house was my station for the next six and a half days. Three and a half hours every morning, scarcely interrupted by a cup of tea, followed by a cycle ride down to Greystones after a bit of lunch; then a tilly of activity for another two and a half hours. That was the day. I had my system worked out for a couple of months beforehand, and it needed only the activity of doing it to make it work. It was based simply on cutting out a cardboard template, onto which I could write the constants and the variables. What was marvellous was that it worked. I made thirty-three mistakes, but detected them all as I made them, and took one day off to go into town to buy thirty-three more newspapers. Thirty-five actually, in case I spoiled any.

I don't know what they thought of me when I came in with my parcel of entries, all correctly filled out and signed, and matched off to postal orders according to their instructions. There was only one instruction I didn't comply with – to post it. I just wouldn't trust the post, or them, in case they might say they didn't receive it. And I waited while the man at the counter phoned upstairs to confirm that he could accept it.

They split the prize fifty-one ways. I don't believe they ever divided it so widely, and I got fourteen pounds fourteen shillings – and I think they may have rounded the pennyha'penny up to thru'ppence or sixpence. I had speculated almost fifty-five quid. I sent them a letter afterwards on the notepaper with my nickname, Jago, printed aslant in Italics in the top left-hand corner. One word only, I wrote: Bastards!

I went around to Galway on the Cu Feasa that year with the intention of quitting after the Fleadh Cheoil. It was to be in Swinford. I found that I had become the centre of focus in those niggling matters that appeared to crop up from time to time; and when Dennis Daly stopped ashore to study for his mates full ticket, I was passed over for the chance of Acting Mate. Billy Glansford who wasn't even a member of the crew, was taken on instead. I planned after the Fleadh, to borrow Lewy O'Rourke's tent and hitchhike around Ireland. After that, I thought, I would walk to China. I had always wanted to see the World, and would start with Europe. A week before the fleadh, I bumped into my brother Billy on Mainguard St.

in Galway. He was in the city for the Sugar Company on some international conference.

"Do you know anything about prawns?" he said, "Do you know they come well out of freeze-drying? The company is interested".

--------------- 0 -------------------------------- 0 ----------------

I first saw her

Across a crowded street in a Connaught market town,

Hair all curling gold;

Light of step she walked with Lewy O'Rourke and Gerry Considine

Friends.

When introduced, she folded her fingers into my proffered hand

And we walked on together

Towards the music.

I did not know then that this young woman, this Ann Barragry,

Would join her life to mine.

I knew only that this was

Fleadh Cheoil

Swinford

Nineteen Sixty-one.

That's how it was.

Jago Hayden.
12.30 P.M., 12th December 1998.